This is my sampler...

The Art Needle

A Handy, Chatty Guide to Art Embroidery Pattern Basics

For nearly a century, a wonderful relaxing pastime entertained women through the U.S. and much of the world. No one thought much of art embroidery while they were doing it; after all, it was just something to pass the time, making a thoughtful gift for a friend or a treat for oneself. So little consideration has been given to this facet of textile history that some experts cringe when they hear "art embroidery" applied to the stamped goods and transfers our mothers and grandmothers bought for a dollar (or a penny!) from the variety store. But "art embroidery" is indeed what the magazines and pattern publishers and catalogues called those frivolous fanciful, frothy designs...so I will, too!

This edition of The Art Needle will give you a little expertise of your own; because while textile historians have been focusing on rarer things, the records and memories of this widely popular needlework have been disintegrating right under our noses. If you want to date your patterns or understand a little more about the general trends of art embroidery, you may find a bit of help here. I wish it could be more.

Of course, this publication is just a thimbleful of ocean. What a rich legacy of ordinary pleasure and simple lives is left unwritten in the fascinating history of art embroidery! Those of you who cherish bluebird-covered dresser scarves and scotties-chasing-kitties tea towels know how compelling is the untold story of the woman who made them. Imagine her story multiplied by millions! That is the scope of art embroidery. Rare because is it so very ordinary, so truly popular, so absolutely basic.

Don't ever doubt that something more than floss was measured out in those stitches. They record as much as a vintage magazine, and still keep secrets only a loved one can decode. If you never hear it anywhere else, at least you heard it here: Those stacks of Colonial Lady pillowcases crammed in your linen cupboard are precious, and not just because of their sentimental or family importance. They let us reach back and touch an ordinary moment in the past, in a way so direct and immediate it can be a little spooky. They tell a history worth hearing; and you are right, right, right to keep listening.

Pincushions, Needlecases & Notions Holders

Computerized sewing machines are all very well, but when it comes to charming and whimsical sewing notions, other generations of women had the advantage over modern stitchers. A glance at mail order catalogs from the 1880s to 1940s reveals an array of enchanting figural and decorative notions that make the red tomato pincushion most of us use look quite dull.

1700s - Like a sailor's compass or an artist's brush, needles & pins were once precious tools. • Too valuable to waste or lose, sewing items were kept in chatelaines, often made to fold entire mending kits, including scissors, thimble and even magnifier into a tiny space. • Highly decorated chatelaines were fashionable accessories for respectable ladies for well over 100 years.

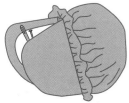

1880-1915 - Pincushions caught the fancy of late Victorians. • Although there were many delightful manufactured pincushions to choose from, a lady of this era might prefer to make her own from instructions in her favorite fancywork column. • Pretty slippers, luxurious chaise lounges or natural shapes, such as acorns and horse chestnuts were created from bits of shirt board, paste, scraps of silk and cotton wadding.

1920-1940 - Jazz Age and Depression Era homemakers had their own version of elaborate pincushions. • Charming cottages, clock faces and sunbonnet babies were just a few of the popular themes transformed into needle cases. • Most styles were made using a few patches of colorful felt and embroidery floss.

1940-1959 - Throughout their history, sewing notion projects have served purposes beyond holding needles, pins and thread. • Because they were small, quickly and easily made, they were perfect for teaching a girl to sew. This lovely idea also rewarded the young seamstress with something she could truly use and treasure forever. • Similarly, ladies' auxiliaries found pincushions and needlebooks desirable items for fund-raising bazaars.

The charm of sewing aids is reflected in our recent fascination for collecting them. Grandmother may have paid a dime for her Sunbonnet Sue needlebook at a church bazaar, we'll spend a few dollars on one today. Felt needlecases from the '20s - '30s are quite affordable to collect, but chatelaines, depending on their rarity and decorative value may range in price from a few hundred dollars to over $2,000!

Bonnet Ladies

A sisterhood representing the very essence of art embroidery, Bonnet Ladies were once found decorating everything from lamp bases to celluloid brooches. Their most enduring and perhaps endearing expression is on pillowcases, dresser scarves and other art embroidery.

1880 - 1915 - Naively styled interpretations of Kate Greenaway's illustrations in the 1800s, which emphasized bonnets over faces. The popular Bertha Corbett's Sunbonnet Babies are the likely origins of Sunbonnet Sue and Overall Bill/Sam style patterns later.

1920s - The Jazz Age fad for colonial furnishings inspired hundreds of Colonial ladies and gents for embroidery, in styles from quaint to courtly, in true American Colonial tradition. The patterns were generally very realistically and richly detailed. • Sunbonnet Sue patterns emerge from Sunbonnet Baby style motifs.

1930s - Sunbonnet Sue becomes entirely distinct from the Colonial Bonnet lady. • Sweeping portrait hats framed Poster ladies, while tiers of sateen created Ribbon Lady pictures. • Crinoline Lady pictures, boudoir pillows and other items incorporate satin ribbons or laces for skirts.

1940 - 1959 - Sunbonnet Sue motifs increase in popularity and detail, especially as Day of the Week towel patterns. • Colonial Ladies become increasingly fanciful; an elongated form and arabesque arms are typical. • The Bonnet Lady grew fashionably thin in the 1940s and 1950s, often incorporating crochet or ruffles for skirts.

Bonnet Ladies were called Crinoline Ladies in the United Kingdom. These Lovely Ladies usually wore full or frilly skirts or aprons. They often donned hats or beautiful bonnets.

Nursery Themes

Art embroidery marks the continuity of generations as well as themes. Nursery motifs are an especially good example of this. Although fashions for baby things did change, the cuddly toys and sweet decorative motifs of the 1950s would have looked quite familiar to a mother from the 1830s.

1880-1915 - Two distinct styles were popular - delicate and formal (usually White-on-White) and whimsical (often Redwork). • Formal baby decorations were indistinguishable from other White-on-White designs. • Whimsical nursery items were generally illustrated with a very realistic style.

1915 - The use of playful designs on children's clothes increases in popularity. • Most baby clothes motifs are still done in White-on-White.• Popular nursery characters from Beatrix Potter's to Sunbonnet Babies copied for embroidery themes.

1920 - Children's clothes were highly decorated with stylish motifs, including whimsical pockets, bibs, etc. • Embroidery combined with fabric tinting on dolls and nursery items. • Realistic style was still common in whimsical motifs. • Stylized illustrations became more popular for children's themes. • Delicate, formal patterns are still popular, but now they might be done in color.

1930 - Tinted fabric with embroidery gains huge popularity, then fades. • Highly stylized animals and other playmates are common whimsical themes. • Patterns for delicate formal stitching still available but not as popular.

1940-1959 - Selection of wearable baby items for embroidery becomes more limited. • Whimsy becomes more restrained, less outlandish. • Themes from the new popular culture - such as cowboys and ballerinas - incorporated.

"Old fashioned designs are the latest fad, yet economical."
- Sadie Le Suere
***Woman's World*, 1928**

Flower Basket Infinity

It is hardly an exaggeration to say that the number of flower basket designs created in the last century for use in art embroidery is impossible to count. While many flower basket designs reveal a style typical of their era, just as many do not. A design from the late 1800s might be virtually indistinguishable from a 1950s basket. Pattern publishers were well aware of this fact and sold many flower basket designs, unaltered, for decades. Talk about shelf life!

1880-1915 - Flower basket designs were rendered down to tiny details. • Each design had dainty proportions. • There was a genuine sense of movement. • Motifs were frequently intended for Whitework. • "Graceful" was an apt description for patterns of this era.

1920 - Linens were shaped to incorporate the basket into the design. • Linking accent shapes were common. • Ingenuity and variety appeared in blossom caricatures. • Baskets were as important as the flowers. • There was generally less exuberant movement in the patterns.

1930 - Designs had more in common with the 1940s and 1950s than with the 1880s and 1920s. • Unique designs featured typical art deco characteristics.

1940-1959 - Patterns were highly detailed, generally filling color into the design. • Designs were static, even where movement was meant to be implied. • Pretty and very feminine defined the era. • There was a uniformity in flower caricatures. • Highly realistic arrangements become increasingly fanciful. • Details embellished designs but were non-essential.

"She sews and dreams of coming happy hours, While 'neath her fingers blossom lovely flowers..."

- Viola Perry Wanger
Home Arts, October, 1936

Children and Cuddle Dolls

Cuddle dolls were a childhood favorite for years. From the 1880s through the 1950s, they were offered both ready-made and as kits. The earliest dolls were lavish lithographed items, often of fairy tale characters, animals or famous people. Beginning after 1900, dolls became simpler embroidered, tinted or appliqued renditions of objects, animals, people and famous personalities.

1880s - The popularity of dolls was due to their ease of construction, durability and adaptability to favorite subjects. • Almost any character or object could be traced from favorite books or illustrations and easily turned into a doll using stitching, applique, painting or often a combination of all three techniques.

1900 - 1950 - Doll kits, along with kits for other stitchery, were readily available from a variety of sources. • Herrschners, Bucilla, Royal Society, Vogart and Coats & Clark were some of the more notable manufacturers. • Most needlework catalogs offered pre-stamped and often pre-tinted muslin dolls, ready for embroidering and assembly.

Present Day - From the pudgy faced Grace Drayton type children to the soldiers and sailors popular during both World Wars, it is easy to see the attraction these dolls have to collectors. They often reflected current events in the form of famous people and characters during any given decade. These historical references made the dolls attractive to both doll collectors and people collecting items pertaining to a given event, person or era. The dolls can be difficult to find today. As with most children's items, there were often used up and thrown away. Early lithographed dolls run well into the hundreds of dollars, especially when related to famous people or event. Later embroidered character and object dolls are common and many have survived. Depending on condition and quality of stitching, these dolls can be found in the range of $20 to $100.

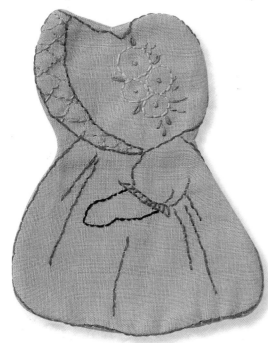

What very small person doesn't love the quaint homemade cuddle toys? They may be squeezed as tight as one likes, or tossed about like a ball, and not a bit of harm done ...they are so soft and snugglesome and altogether adorable, and so easy, withal, for tiny hands to hold."

- Viola Perry Wanger
Needlecraft 1923

Kitchen Stitchin' & Days of the Week

Art embroidery for the kitchen, because of its often whimsical basis, provided designers with rich opportunities to explore favorite themes for 'Days of the Week' tea towels again and again.

1880-1915 - Utilitarian kitchen themes were favored. • Realistic, elegant renderings of tableware, cookware, glassware, fruits and meats were the most common. • Whimsical items, such as elves with fruit or humorous laundry bags were included as popular themes.

1920s - Whimsical kitchen themes became increasingly popular by the end of the decade. • Style combines realistic items, such as glassware or china, with rudimentary human features. • Realistic kitchen themes continue to be very popular motifs.

1930s - Humorous kitchen themes gained even greater appeal during this decade. • The Depression focus was on creativity and useful fancies such as elaborate potholder kits. • 'Days of the Week' towels became common with Sunbonnet Sue, related characters and daily chores used as the most frequent themes.

1940-1959 - 'Days of the Week' towels gained even greater popularity. • The most common themes were animals (such as dogs, cats and chickens), Sunbonnet Sue, vegetable and chinaware personalities. • Clever details (period washing machines, etc.) added distinction. • Realistic themes were still offered. • War-time frugality continued the demand for ingenious scrap projects like potholders. • Style was very exuberant, genuinely witty - no holds barred! • Unique themes ranged from a pooped housewife to a spaceman. • The mid- and late 1950s brought a more restrained style, fewer novel details, and greater detail rendering facial expressions.

No matter the era, women used their leisure time to add a touch of whimsy, beauty or humor to their surroundings. This had to help hurry along everyday chores and must have lightened the load.

The subjects and styles have changed a bit over the years.

The ethnic stereotypes, once so popular, have thankfully gone by the way. To give a true survey of needlework from this century, a few of those stereotypes have been added to this book. They are also a part of our heritage.

Ladies Quilt

FINISHED SIZE: 72" x 83"

MATERIALS:
- 44" wide, 100% cotton fabrics:
  $2^1/4$ yards White fabric for blocks
  $7^1/2$ yards Blue fabric for blocks, borders and backing
- Thirty 11" squares of assorted fabrics for the appliques
- 77" x 88" piece of batting
- Skeins of assorted embroidery flosses to coordinate with the applique fabrics
- Blue and White sewing threads

CUTTING:
- Cut 21 White $11^1/2$" squares.
- Cut 21 Blue $11^1/2$" squares.
- Cut 2 Blue 3" x $66^1/2$" strips for the top and bottom borders.
- Cut 2 Blue 3" x 83" strips for the side borders.
- Cut 2 Blue 39" x 88" pieces for the backing.
- Cut Blue $1^1/4$" strips for binding.

DESIGN BLOCKS:
Transfer the design on page 43 to each of the assorted fabric squares. Cut along the dotted line. Turn back the seam allowance and trim curves as necessary. Pin or baste the design onto the center of a White square. Use 2 strands of floss to blanket stitch the edges in place. Remove the basting stitches or pins. Stitch details and flowers Press each square.

These ladies may not really 'walk' in beauty like the night, but they'll be there to keep you warm while you sleep!

ASSEMBLY:
1. Use $1/4$" seam allowances throughout.
2. With right sides facing, sew 3 Blue squares alternating with 3 White squares to make 4 rows. Press the seams toward the Blue squares. Sew 3 White squares alternately with 3 Blue squares to make 3 rows. Press the seams toward the Blue squares.

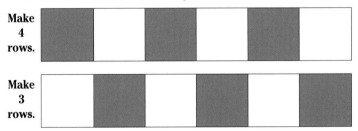

Make 4 rows.

Make 3 rows.

3. With right sides facing, sew the alternating rows together as shown in the Assembly Diagram. Press seams open.
4. With right sides facing, sew the Blue top and bottom border strips in place. Press the seams toward the border strips.
5. With right sides facing, sew the Blue side border strips in place. Press seams toward the border strips.
6. With right sides facing, sew the 2 Blue backing pieces together down the center long edge. Press the seam open.
7. Layer the backing, batting and the assembled top to form a sandwich. Center the top on the batting. Baste the layers together.
8. Quilt the quilt as desired.
9. Remove the basting stitches. Trim the backing and batting even with the edges of the quilt top.
10. Bind the edges with the Blue $1^1/4$" strips. With right sides facing, sew strip ends together. Press seams open. Sew strips to back of quilt, fold back $1/4$" along raw edge. Fold over, whip stitch in place.

LADIES QUILT ASSEMBLY DIAGRAM

Bonnie Bonnet Girls Quilt

FINISHED SIZE: 67" x 79"

MATERIALS:

- 44" wide, 100% cotton fabrics:
  7 yards White fabric for blocks and backing
  2¼ yards Lavender fabric for the sashing strips and borders
  Thirty 7" squares of assorted fabrics for the appliqued dresses
  Thirty 7" squares of assorted fabrics to coordinate with the dress fabrics for the hats, arms and shoes
  ¼ yard of Pink fabric for the appliqued hands
- 71" x 84" piece of batting
- Skeins of assorted embroidery flosses to coordinate with the applique fabrics
- White sewing thread

CUTTING:

- Cut 30 White 10½" squares.
- Cut 4 Lavender 3½" x 75½" pieces for the vertical sashing strips.
- Cut 25 Lavender 3½" x 10½" strips for the horizontal sashing strips.
- Cut 2 Lavender 2¼" x 75½" strips for the side borders.
- Cut 2 Lavender 2¼" x 66½" strips for the top and bottom borders.
- Cut 2 White 36" x 84" pieces for the backing.

DESIGN BLOCKS:

Transfer the dress, hat, arm and shoe designs on page 81 to the assorted fabrics squares. Transfer and cut 30 Pink hands. Cut along the dotted line. Turn back the seam allowance and trim curves as necessary. Pin or baste the shapes onto the center of a White square. Build the design up in layers. Begin with the shoe, add the dress, hand, arm and end with the hat. Use 2 strands of coordinating floss to blanket stitch the edges in place. Remove the basting stitches or pins. Cross stitch the hatband. Press each square.

ASSEMBLY:

1. Use ¼" seam allowances throughout.
2. With right sides facing, sew 5 Lavender horizontal sashing strips alternating with 6 White squares to make 5 rows. Press the seams toward the Lavender strips.
3. With right sides facing, sew the Lavender vertical sashing strips between the block rows as shown in the Assembly Diagram. Press the seams open.
4. With right sides facing, sew the Lavender side border strips in place. Press seams toward the border strips.
5. With right sides facing, sew the Lavender top and bottom border strips in place. Press the seams toward the border strips.
6. With right sides facing, sew the 2 White backing pieces together down the center long edge. Press the seam open.
7. Layer the backing, batting and the assembled top to form a sandwich. Center the top on the batting. Baste the layers together.
8. Quilt the quilt as desired.
9. Remove the basting stitches. Trim the batting even with the edges of the quilt top. Cut the backing 1" larger than the quilt top and batting around all edges. Fold up ¼" along each side of the backing. Press. Fold the edge over to form a ¾" binding. Whip stitch the edges in place. Repeat across the top and bottom edges.

This Sunbonnet Sue quilt proves that Sue had a different outfit for every day of the month. What a great way to use up scraps!

BONNET GIRLS QUILT ASSEMBLY DIAGRAM

Big Golden Butterflies Quilt

FINISHED SIZE: 68" x 88"

MATERIALS:
- 44" wide, 100% cotton fabrics:
  9 yards White fabric for blocks and backing
  4 yards Yellow fabric for the sashing strips, borders and appliques
- 74" x 94" piece of batting
- 3 skeins of Black embroidery floss
- White sewing thread

CUTTING:
- Cut 12 White 17" x 17" squares for embroidery.
- Cut 2 Yellow $3^1/2$" x $75^1/2$" pieces for the center vertical sashing strips.
- Cut 4 Yellow $3^1/2$" x $75^1/2$" strips for the side borders.
- Cut 4 Yellow $3^1/2$" x 68" pieces for the top and bottom border strips.
- Cut 9 Yellow $3^1/2$" x 17" horizontal sashing strips.
- Cut 2 White $37^1/4$" x 94" pieces for the backing.
- Cut White $1^1/4$" strips for the quilt binding.

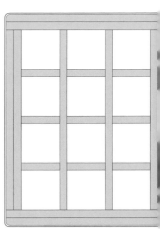

**YELLOW BUTTERFLIES QUILT
ASSEMBLY DIAGRAM**

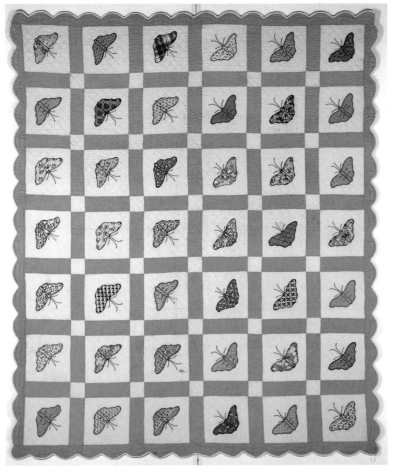

Small Multicolor Butterflies Quilt

FINISHED SIZE: 75" x 87"
MATERIALS:
- 44" wide, 100% cotton fabrics:
  $9^1/2$ yards White fabric for blocks and backing
  $2^1/4$ yards Pink fabric for the sashing strips and borders
- Forty-two 4" x 8" squares of assorted fabrics for appliques
- 80" x 92" piece of batting
- 3 skeins of Black embroidery floss
- White sewing thread
- $7^1/2$" plate to mark the scallops

CUTTING:
- Cut 42 White $9^1/2$" squares.
- Cut 3 White $3^1/2$" x 42" pieces for the sashing strips.
- Cut 7 Pink $9^1/2$" x 42" pieces for the sashing strips.
- Cut 2 Pink $3^1/2$" x $81^1/2$" strips for the side borders.
- Cut 2 Pink $3^1/2$" x 75" top and bottom border strips.
- Cut 41 Pink $3^1/2$" x $9^1/2$" horizontal sashing strips.
- Cut 2 White $40^1/2$" x 92" pieces for the backing.
- Cut White $1^1/4$" strips for the binding.

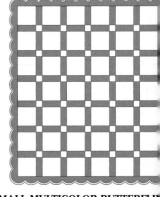

**SMALL MULTICOLOR BUTTERFLI[ES]
QUILT ASSEMBLY DIAGRAM**

DESIGN BLOCKS:

Transfer the butterfly wing and body designs on page 28 to the remaining piece of Yellow fabric. Cut the wings on the fold. Cut along the dotted line. Turn back the seam allowance and trim curves as necessary. Pin or baste the wings onto the center of a White square. Secure the body on top. Use 2 strands of floss to blanket stitch the edges in place. Remove the basting stitches or pins. Stitch the remaining details, alternating wing styles. Press squares.

ASSEMBLY:

1. Use $1/4$" seam allowances throughout.
2. With right sides facing, sew 3 Yellow horizontal sashing strips alternating with 4 White squares to make 3 rows. Press the seams toward the Yellow strips.
3. With right sides facing, sew the Yellow vertical sashing strips between the block rows as shown in the Assembly Diagram. Press the seams toward the Yellow strips.
4. With right sides facing, sew the Yellow side border strips in place. Press the seams toward the border strips.
5. With right sides facing, sew the Yellow top and bottom border strips in place. Press all the seams toward the Yellow border strips.
6. With right sides facing, sew the 2 White backing pieces together down the center long edge. Press the seam open.
7. Layer the backing, batting and the assembled top to form a sandwich. Center the top on the batting. Baste all of the layers together.
8. Quilt the quilt as desired.
9. Remove the basting stitches. Trim the batting even with the edges of the quilt top. Round the corners of the quilt, if desired. Use a plate edge for uniform curves.
10. Bind the edges with the White $1^1/4$" strips.

DESIGN BLOCKS:

Transfer the butterfly designs on page 29 to the squares of assorted fabrics. Follow the instructions for Design Blocks, above, to cut and pin or baste and attach each design at an angle onto a White square. Press squares.

ASSEMBLY:

1. Use $1/4$" seam allowances throughout.
2. Cut 4 of the Pink sashing strips into pieces $3^1/2$" wide. Sew 6 butterfly blocks alternately with 5 Pink strips to form 7 rows. Press seams toward the Pink strips.
3. With right sides facing, sew a White $3^1/2$" sashing strip to one side of a $9^1/2$" Pink strip. Press seams open. Cut each set into pieces $3^1/2$" wide. Repeat with the remaining White and Pink strips. Sew 5 Pink/White sets with a Pink piece to form 6 horizontal sashing rows. Press seams open. Sew these sashing strips between the block rows as shown in the Assembly Diagram. Press seams open.
4. With right sides facing, sew the Pink side border strips in place. Press the seams toward the border strips.
5. With right sides facing, sew the Pink top and bottom border strips in place. Press seams toward the border strips.
6. Begin at one corner to draw scallops on quilt top. Scallops should be 3" deep, $5^1/2$" wide. The points between the scallops is $1^3/4$" deep.
7. With right sides facing, sew the 2 White backing pieces together down the center long edge. Press the seam open.
8. Layer the backing, batting and the assembled top to form a sandwich. Center the top on the batting. Baste all of the layers together. Quilt the quilt as desired.
9. Remove the basting stitches. Trim edges of the quilt layers along the scallop lines. Bind edges with the White strips.

Care of Linens

As vintage linens have become more collectible, many enthusiasts have become textile conservators to their own mini-museums of heirloom dresser scarves, doilies and Days-of-the-week towels. It isn't hard or expensive to store and clean a collection safely, if you take advantage of some common sense - and some new products.

Roll linens to prevent ironing them!

Rolling linens for storage, like Grandma did, was so widely practiced that embroidery kits for decorative linen rolls were popular sellers in turn-of-the-century catalogs! Today, textile experts heartily endorse Grandma's method. Placing a piece of acid-free tissue on the surface of the textile will reduce wrinkles even further. From a practical point of view, rolling may not always be possible. Make sure your most precious linens get this treatment. If you must fold, use acid-free tissue and fold the piece in thirds, not halves. At least creases won't run right through the middle of the piece.

Acid-free cardboard comes to the rescue!

Conservators highly recommend the use of acid-free cardboard to store almost everything - including linens. Why? Air circulation is important to prevent moisture damage - a common culprit when storing textiles. See-through plastic containers, though, are convenient, affordable and available. If you are going to store in plastic, keep the containers away from damp, open them regularly and line them with acid free tissue. Indulge in the pleasure of examining your collection often, but wear white cotton gloves to keep from adding moisture from your hands.

Think before you wash - or sink!

Conservators view washing as a last resort for restoring the look of linens. Simply airing textiles to remove musty smells is far safer than washing will ever be - and it's definitely the first step to try. Several products, available at some antique stores, are specially designed for removing 'yellowing' and 'light stains' from linens. Never use an, untried product on a treasured heirloom! Try the product out on a few "disposable" vintage scraps to test its stain removal abilities and damage potential.

Modern science vs. the kitchen cupboard!

Many antique dealers and quilt shops carry stain removers formulated especially to remove age spots from antique linens. Homemade formulas abound, as well. A solution of equal parts of 'Biz' and 'Cascade' has many loyal users, as does baking soda and lemon juice. Remember that washing is only half the battle - rinsing is equally important, since detergent residue actually attracts dirt and oil to fibers. After rinsing, smooth the article carefully on a towel and roll gently to press out moisture. Never, ever wring an heirloom textile item! Lay the piece flat to dry, unless you really don't care if the item is permanently stretched out of shape.

Harness the sun for good - not evil!

Mildew stains can be bleached somewhat from white linens by washing them and drying them flat in sunshine. But beware! Direct sunlight is guaranteed to fade any colored textile or embroidery. If your heart is set on cafe curtains from old printed tablecloths, resign yourself to seeing their bright colors fade over time. Glass and sunlight are another combination that textile guardians caution against. A good framer knows to recommend plexiglass or a glass that screens ultraviolet rays when framing your heirloom embroidery.

Styles 100 years in 100 words or less.

A tip-of-the iceberg, seat-of-your-pants synopsis of the basic trends of art embroidery patterns.

 *1880 - 1900* - Realistic or naturalistic renderings. • Visual puns and symbolic messages common. • "Talking" linens with greetings or jokes. • Novelty work done in strong, natural colors. • Fine embroidery used for better quality decorative purposes - eyeletting, padded satin stitch, etc. • Turkey work/Redwork a popular trend, where patterns for Kensington stitch (needlepainting) were done in outlining only, in Turkey Red. • First iron-on transfers appear on the market. • Bonanza of easily available flosses, fabrics and patterns suddenly became available.

 *1900 - 1910* - Arts & Crafts style patterns are a special niche in the kit and pattern market. • Simplified natural forms (flowers and abstract forms) often combine some very curvlinear elements of art nouveau. • Many kits pre-tinted to show elaborate stitching plans. This tinting was often simply outlined and left to be enjoyed on its own.

 1900 - 1920 - Novelty patterns become increasingly professional looking. • Novelty motifs continue to be increasingly realistic. • Fine embroidery motifs continue in eyeletting and other traditional methods.

 *1920s* - Kits for embroidered everything, from clothes to umbrella holders, were available. • Incredible number of patterns published. It's a golden era for art embroidery. • Linens featured unusually-shaped edges and corners, often fitting tightly to motifs. • Colonial Lady themes began popularity. • There was increasing whimsy and stylization in many designs. • Black highlights and accents were common in light pastel color schemes. • Tinting became increasingly common in combination with embroidery.

 *1930s* - Patterns were highly professional, standardized. • Motifs tended toward lush shapes, colors or backgrounds. • Boudoir pillows, potholders and Day of the Week towels became increasingly popular. • Novelty dolls, pajama bags and other objects combined tinting, sewing and embroidery. • Styles were influenced by Art Deco - strong shapes and luxurious colors. Black was used as a background color for a stark, rich effect.

 *1940s* - War conscious patterns appeared, including stuffed soldier dolls and motifs of soldiers with girls, etc • Patterns took on slightly cartooned features, such as chipmunk cheeks and especially large eyes, on a consistent basis, similar to other cartoon artwork of the period. • Variety of shapes in linens decreased, leading to less complex hems and finishing. • Period details were commonly used to add life to patterns. • Increasingly refined patterns mimicked the real world, but always as a caricature.

1950 - 1960 - Patterns moved from highly rendered to occasionally over-rendered (action lines, etc.) complicated patterns. • Period details were no longer found. • There were fewer pattern publishers to choose among. • Elaborately feminine designs featured figures and lines consistent with the elegant fashions of the times.

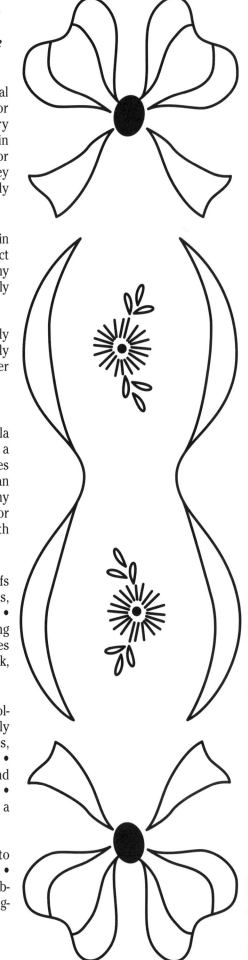

ASSEMBLY: Use ¹/₄" seam allowance throughout.

With right sides facing, sew across the top of the Dog Back. Clip curves as necessary. Lay piece flat. Cut the slit for the tail.

With right sides facing, sew Dog Belly to Dog Back, aligning dots. Leave an opening along one side to stuff.

Stuff the leg area at one end of the body firmly with fiberfill. Insert a small retractable measuring tape into the center of the body. Push the end of the tape through the tail slit. Glue several strands of Gold yarn to the end of the tape and glue a ¹/₂" piece of Red felt around the end of the tape.

Stuff remainder of body. Sew opening closed.

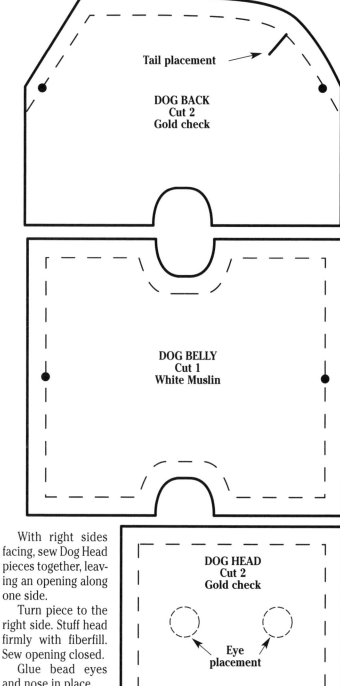

Tail placement

DOG BACK
Cut 2
Gold check

DOG BELLY
Cut 1
White Muslin

With right sides facing, sew Dog Head pieces together, leaving an opening along one side.

Turn piece to the right side. Stuff head firmly with fiberfill. Sew opening closed.

Glue bead eyes and nose in place.

Glue a Gold ¹/₄" pompon above each eye and glue one below the nose.

Sew back of head to neck area of body.

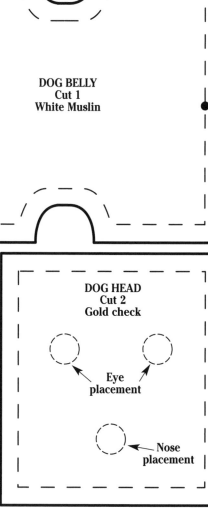

DOG HEAD
Cut 2
Gold check

Eye placement

Nose placement

PHOTOS ON PAGE 5

ASSEMBLY: Blanket stitch outer edges of front, back and roof together around top.

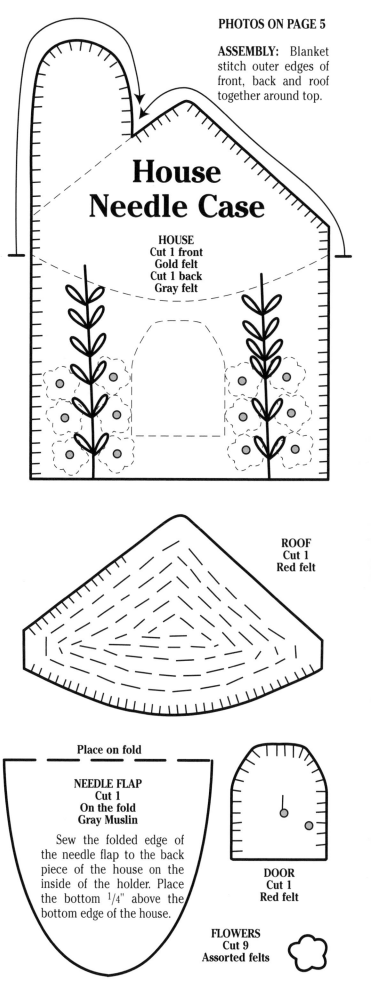

House Needle Case

HOUSE
Cut 1 front
Gold felt
Cut 1 back
Gray felt

ROOF
Cut 1
Red felt

Place on fold

NEEDLE FLAP
Cut 1
On the fold
Gray Muslin

Sew the folded edge of the needle flap to the back piece of the house on the inside of the holder. Place the bottom ¹/₄" above the bottom edge of the house.

DOOR
Cut 1
Red felt

FLOWERS
Cut 9
Assorted felts

Bow placement

Gathered circle of ³/₈" lace

FRONT
Cut 1 - Blue felt
Without feet
BACK
Cut 1 - Blue felt
With feet

FRONT
Cut 1 - Gold felt
Without feet
BACK
Cut 1 - Gold felt
With feet

Button placement
(Sew 1 on back and 1 on front.)

Needle flap placement

Needle flap placement

Gather lace above feet on the back piece.

NEEDLE FLAP
Cut 1
Ivory felt

ARM
Cut 1
Gold felt

NEEDLE FLAP
Cut 1
Gold felt

Gather ³/₈" lace

Gather ³/₈" lace

Collection of 'Sunbonnet Sue' Needle Cases

*"We are the
sunbonnet babies,
Good morning and
how do you do?"*

Eulalie Osgood Grover

Sew the top edge of each of the needle flaps to the back piece of the needlecase according to the placement shown on the patterns.

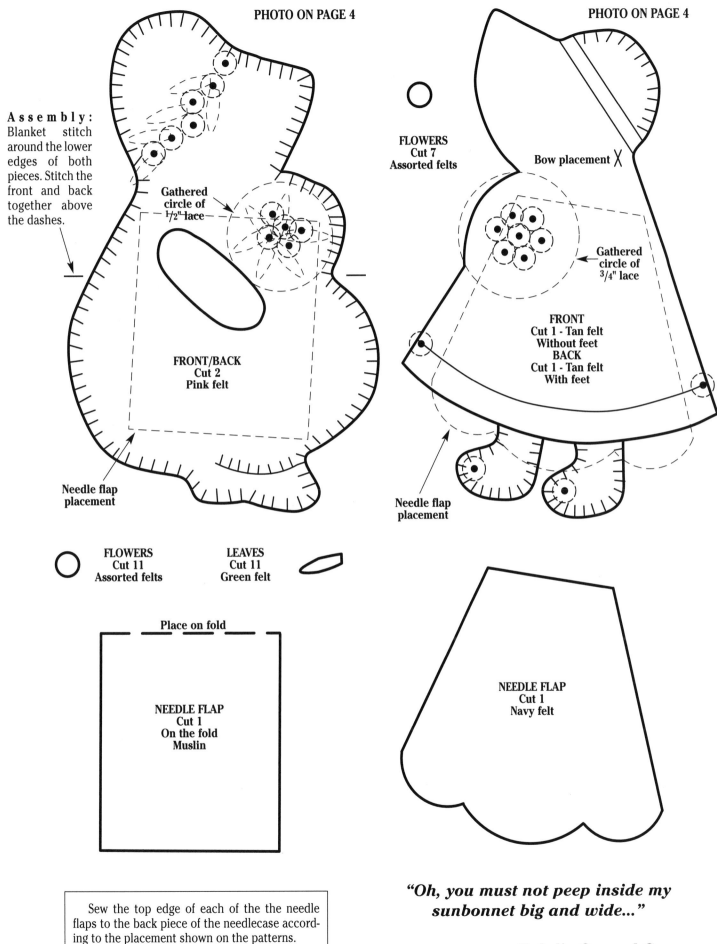

PHOTO ON PAGE 4

Assembly:
Blanket stitch around the lower edges of both pieces. Stitch the front and back together above the dashes.

Gathered circle of 1/2" lace

FRONT/BACK
Cut 2
Pink felt

Needle flap placement

FLOWERS
Cut 7
Assorted felts

Bow placement X

Gathered circle of 3/4" lace

FRONT
Cut 1 - Tan felt
Without feet
BACK
Cut 1 - Tan felt
With feet

Needle flap placement

FLOWERS
Cut 11
Assorted felts

LEAVES
Cut 11
Green felt

Place on fold

NEEDLE FLAP
Cut 1
On the fold
Muslin

NEEDLE FLAP
Cut 1
Navy felt

Sew the top edge of each of the the needle flaps to the back piece of the needlecase according to the placement shown on the patterns.

"Oh, you must not peep inside my sunbonnet big and wide..."

Eulalie Osgood Grover

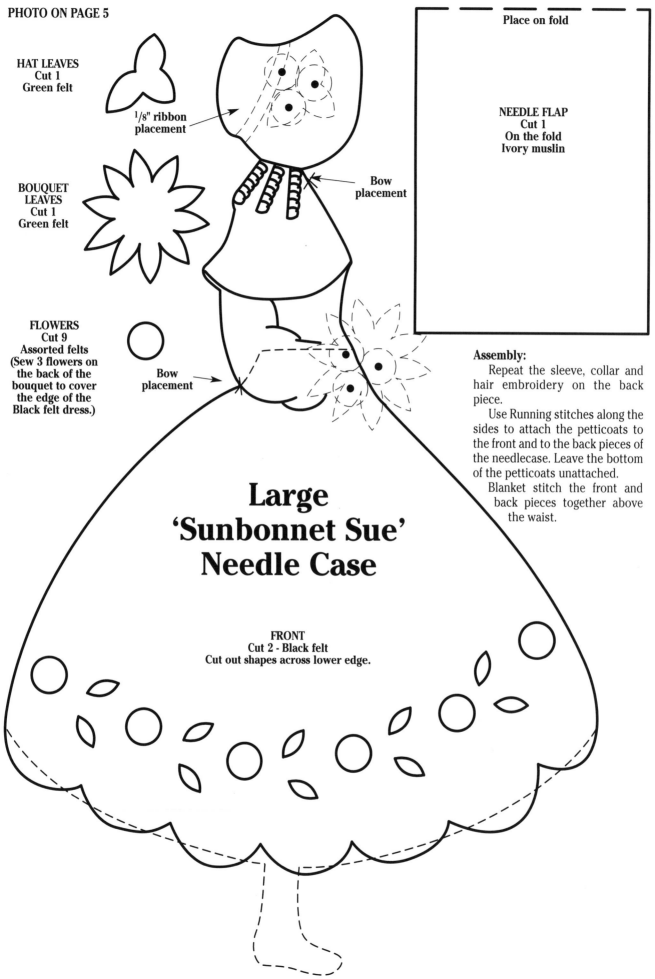

HAT LEAVES
Cut 1
Green felt

¹/₈" ribbon
placement

**BOUQUET
LEAVES**
Cut 1
Green felt

FLOWERS
Cut 9
Assorted felts
(Sew 3 flowers on
the back of the
bouquet to cover
the edge of the
Black felt dress.)

Bow
placement

Place on fold

NEEDLE FLAP
Cut 1
On the fold
Ivory muslin

Bow
placement

Assembly:

Repeat the sleeve, collar and hair embroidery on the back piece.

Use Running stitches along the sides to attach the petticoats to the front and to the back pieces of the needlecase. Leave the bottom of the petticoats unattached.

Blanket stitch the front and back pieces together above the waist.

Large
'Sunbonnet Sue'
Needle Case

FRONT
Cut 2 - Black felt
Cut out shapes across lower edge.

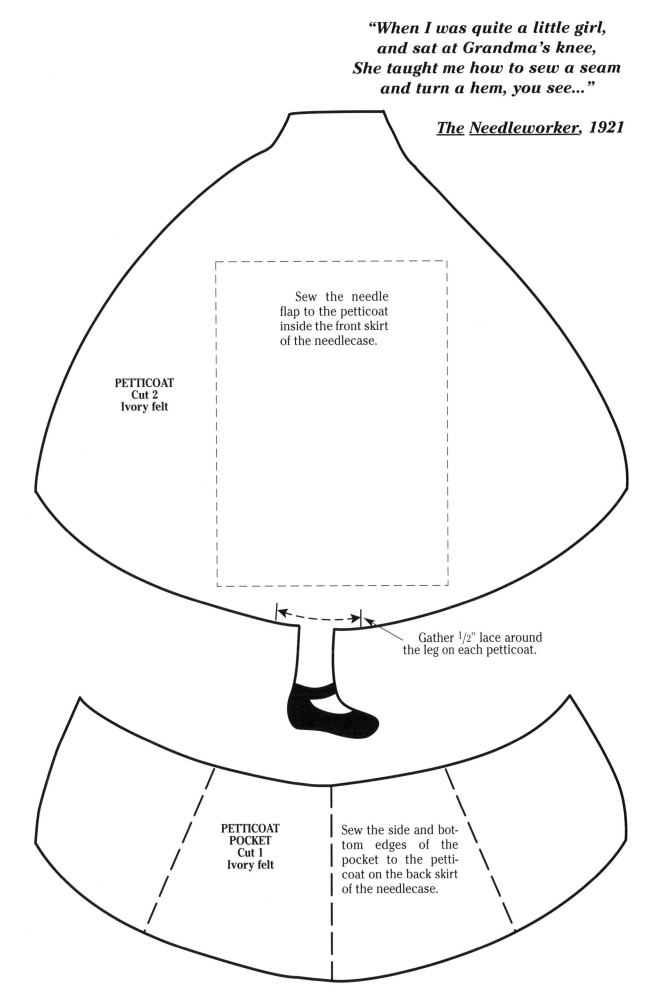

*"When I was quite a little girl,
and sat at Grandma's knee,
She taught me how to sew a seam
and turn a hem, you see..."*

The Needleworker, 1921

Sew the needle
flap to the petticoat
inside the front skirt
of the needlecase.

PETTICOAT
Cut 2
Ivory felt

Gather ¹/₂" lace around
the leg on each petticoat.

PETTICOAT
POCKET
Cut 1
Ivory felt

Sew the side and bot-
tom edges of the
pocket to the petti-
coat on the back skirt
of the needlecase.

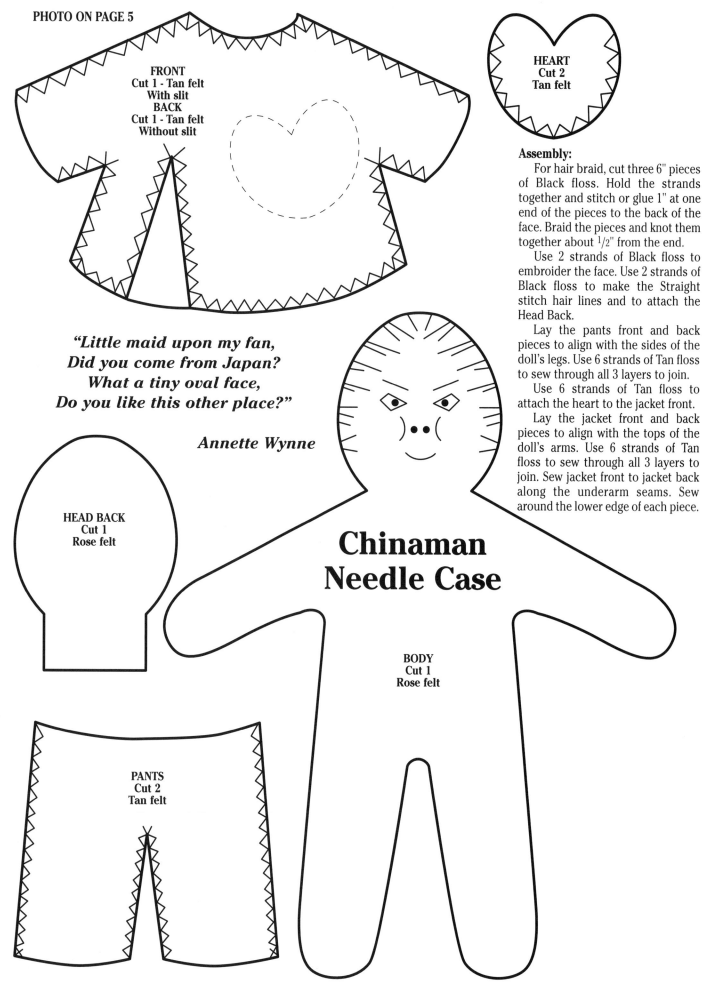

FRONT
Cut 1 - Tan felt
With slit
BACK
Cut 1 - Tan felt
Without slit

HEART
Cut 2
Tan felt

"Little maid upon my fan,
Did you come from Japan?
What a tiny oval face,
Do you like this other place?"

Annette Wynne

HEAD BACK
Cut 1
Rose felt

Chinaman Needle Case

BODY
Cut 1
Rose felt

PANTS
Cut 2
Tan felt

Assembly:

For hair braid, cut three 6" pieces of Black floss. Hold the strands together and stitch or glue 1" at one end of the pieces to the back of the face. Braid the pieces and knot them together about 1/2" from the end.

Use 2 strands of Black floss to embroider the face. Use 2 strands of Black floss to make the Straight stitch hair lines and to attach the Head Back.

Lay the pants front and back pieces to align with the sides of the doll's legs. Use 6 strands of Tan floss to sew through all 3 layers to join.

Use 6 strands of Tan floss to attach the heart to the jacket front.

Lay the jacket front and back pieces to align with the tops of the doll's arms. Use 6 strands of Tan floss to sew through all 3 layers to join. Sew jacket front to jacket back along the underarm seams. Sew around the lower edge of each piece.

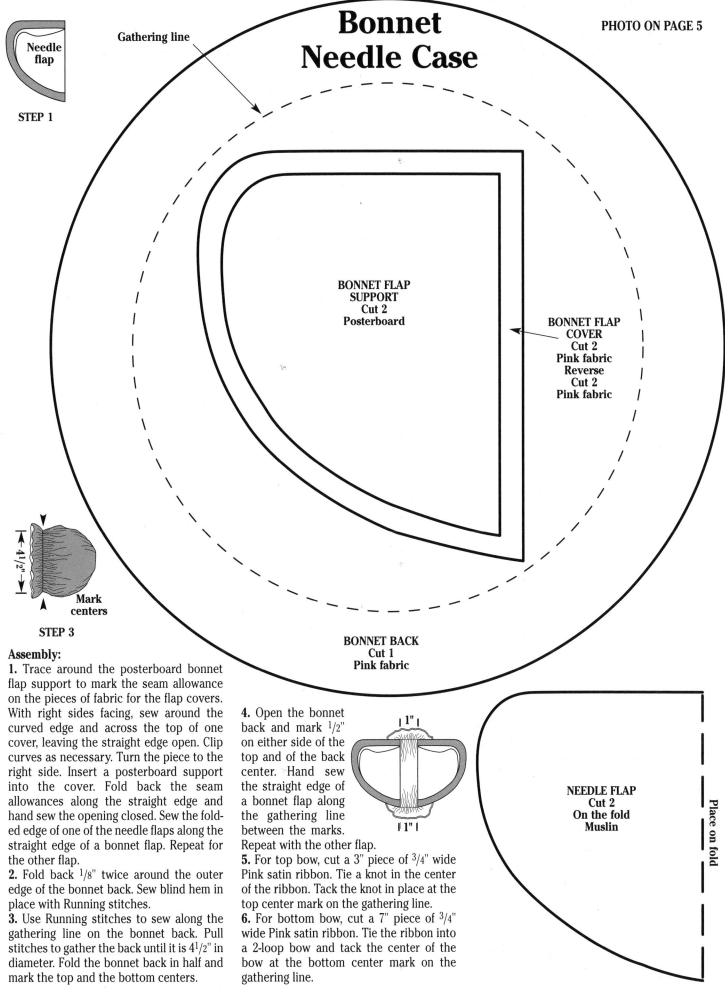

Needle flap

STEP 1

Gathering line

Bonnet Needle Case

PHOTO ON PAGE 5

BONNET FLAP
SUPPORT
Cut 2
Posterboard

BONNET FLAP
COVER
Cut 2
Pink fabric
Reverse
Cut 2
Pink fabric

4½"

Mark centers

STEP 3

BONNET BACK
Cut 1
Pink fabric

NEEDLE FLAP
Cut 2
On the fold
Muslin

Place on fold

1"

1"

Assembly:

1. Trace around the posterboard bonnet flap support to mark the seam allowance on the pieces of fabric for the flap covers. With right sides facing, sew around the curved edge and across the top of one cover, leaving the straight edge open. Clip curves as necessary. Turn the piece to the right side. Insert a posterboard support into the cover. Fold back the seam allowances along the straight edge and hand sew the opening closed. Sew the folded edge of one of the needle flaps along the straight edge of a bonnet flap. Repeat for the other flap.

2. Fold back ⅛" twice around the outer edge of the bonnet back. Sew blind hem in place with Running stitches.

3. Use Running stitches to sew along the gathering line on the bonnet back. Pull stitches to gather the back until it is 4½" in diameter. Fold the bonnet back in half and mark the top and the bottom centers.

4. Open the bonnet back and mark ½" on either side of the top and of the back center. Hand sew the straight edge of a bonnet flap along the gathering line between the marks. Repeat with the other flap.

5. For top bow, cut a 3" piece of ¾" wide Pink satin ribbon. Tie a knot in the center of the ribbon. Tack the knot in place at the top center mark on the gathering line.

6. For bottom bow, cut a 7" piece of ¾" wide Pink satin ribbon. Tie the ribbon into a 2-loop bow and tack the center of the bow at the bottom center mark on the gathering line.

CENTER - Place on fold

Yellow Butterfly Quilt

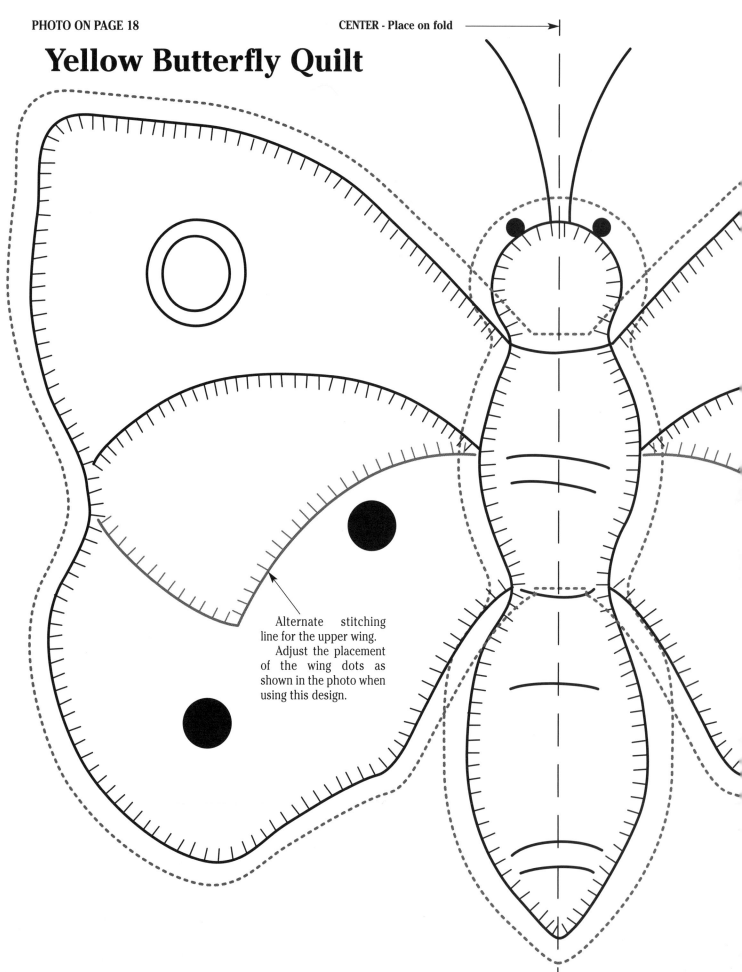

Alternate stitching line for the upper wing. Adjust the placement of the wing dots as shown in the photo when using this design.

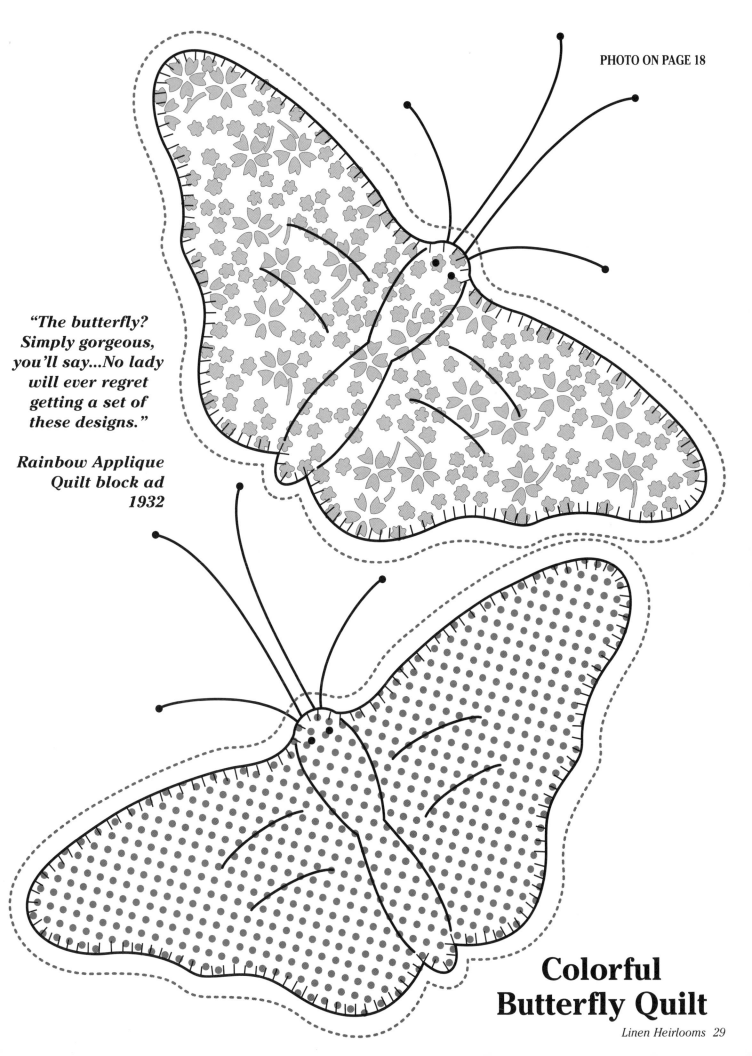

PHOTO ON PAGE 18

*"The butterfly?
Simply gorgeous,
you'll say...No lady
will ever regret
getting a set of
these designs."*

*Rainbow Applique
Quilt block ad
1932*

Colorful
Butterfly Quilt

Care of Linens

Washing

- Test for colorfastness on the seam allowance. Let several drops of water fall through fabric onto white blotter paper. If color appears, the fabric is not colorfast.
- To set dye, soak fabric in water and vinegar.
- Wash in very mild detergent or soap or using tepid water. Follow all label instructions carefully.
- Do not use chlorine bleach on fine linen. Whiten by hanging in full sunlight.

Stain Removal

- Grease - Use a presoak fabric and wash in cold water.
- Nongreasy - Soak in cold water to neutralize. Apply a presoak and wash in cold water.
- Ballpoint Ink - Place on an absorbent material and soak with denatured or rubbing alcohol. Apply room temperature glycerin and flush with water. Finally, apply ammonia and quickly flush with water.
- Candle Wax - Place fabric between layers of absorbent paper and iron on low setting. Change paper as it absorbs wax. If a stained remains wash with peroxy bleach.
- Rust - Remove with lemon juice, oxalic acid or hydrofluoric acid.

Storage

- Wash and rinse thoroughly in soft water.
- Do not size or starch.
- Place cleaned linen on acid free tissue paper and roll loosely.
- Line storage box with layer of acid free paper.
- Placed rolled linens in box. Do not stack. Weight will make creases.
- Do not store linens in plastic bags.
- Hang linen clothing in a muslin bag or cover with a cotton sheet.

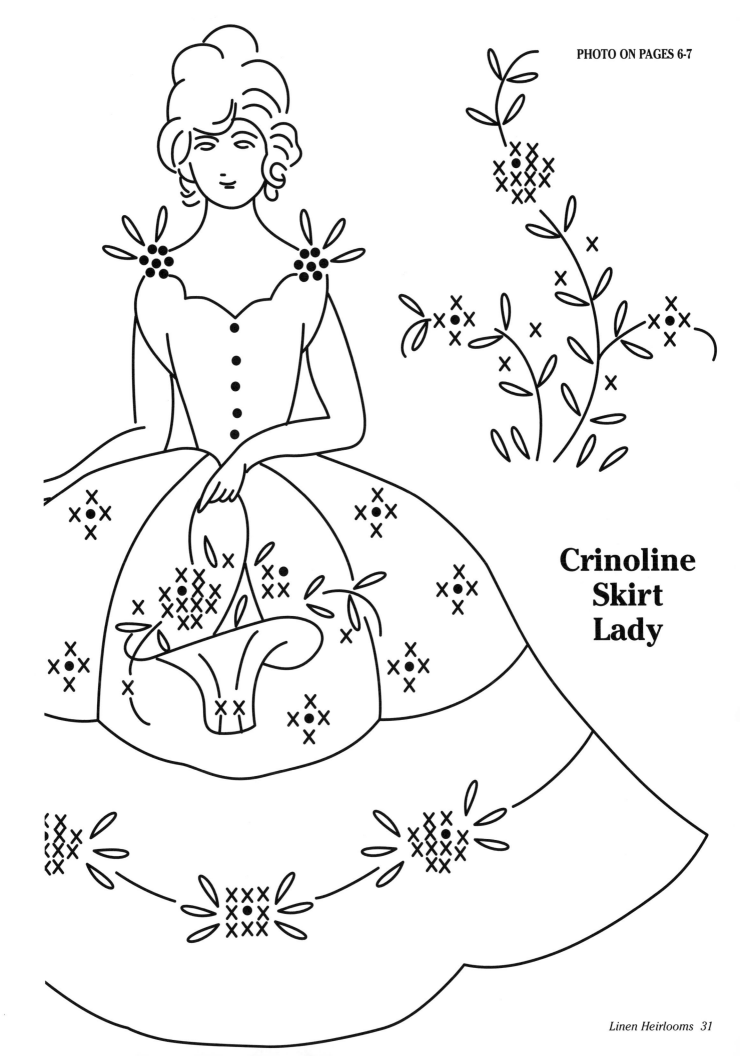

Crinoline Skirt Lady

**Crinoline
Skirt
Girl
with
Umbrella**

*"Be it upstairs or downstairs,
Milady's chamber needs just
such dainty things."*
Modern Priscilla
1919

*"I think, perhaps, that you love me,
But just to be quite sure,
I must show off my homely arts,
These things that will endure."*

Catherine E. Berry

Crinoline Lady with Poppies

Traditional Tinting Technique -

• Use crayons to color the portion of the pattern that you wish to tint.

• Color evenly and smoothly.

• Gently brush away any flakes of color that may accumulate outside the area to be tinted. (These will set into the fabric as little dots of color.

• Place a piece of paper onto the ironing board to protect it from being tinted, too.

• Lay the tinted area of the design on top of the paper.

• Lay another piece of paper on top of the tinted area of the design to protect the sole plate of your iron.

• Use a warm setting with a dry iron to melt the wax of the crayons and to bond the color into the fabric.

PHOTO ON PAGES 6-7

Lady in an Apron

Refer to the instructions on page 35 to tint areas of the design.

*"Even when she isn't there,
her presence fills her room;
As delicate and sweet and fair
as summer's fragrant blooms."*

**Constance Vivien Frazier
<u>Needlecraft</u>, 1937**

Cooking in the Kitchen

Elegant Lady

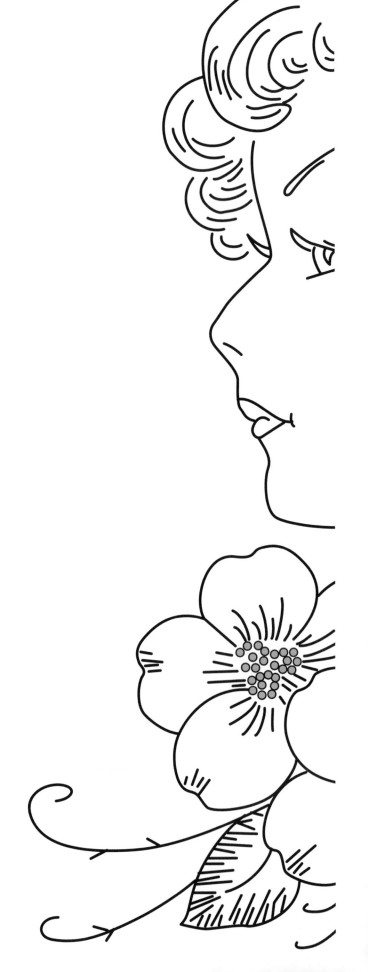

"Dear little girl with the wistful eyes,
Wouldn't you think it a fine surprise,
If the story you loved best came true?"

Then let's get brushes and needle
and thread, And tell it in pictures
on pillow and spread!"

Here's a trivia list of interesting words
you may or may not already know.

Tidies - Term used in the 1800s to describe miscellaneous doilies.

Splashers - Linens placed behind or under a washbowl and basin.

Twist - Turn-of-the-century term for floss, especially filoselle.

Kensington Stitch - A long stitch named for the famous Kensington School of Embroidery.

Art Embroidery - Term used for fancy work after the mid-1890s.

Redwork/Turkeywork - Red outline stitch; substituted for Kensington Stitch.

Needle painting - Fad for realistically embroidered floral motifs.

Popular - Term meaning "of or relating to the general public."

Refer to the instructions on page 35 to tint areas of the design.

**Girl
with
Hat**

Border Design

"Women cannot repress their delight with this lovely pillow."

Richardson Silk Company ad Modern Priscilla 1914

Lady
on the
Edge

PHOTO ON PAGE 16

Crinoline Lady Applique

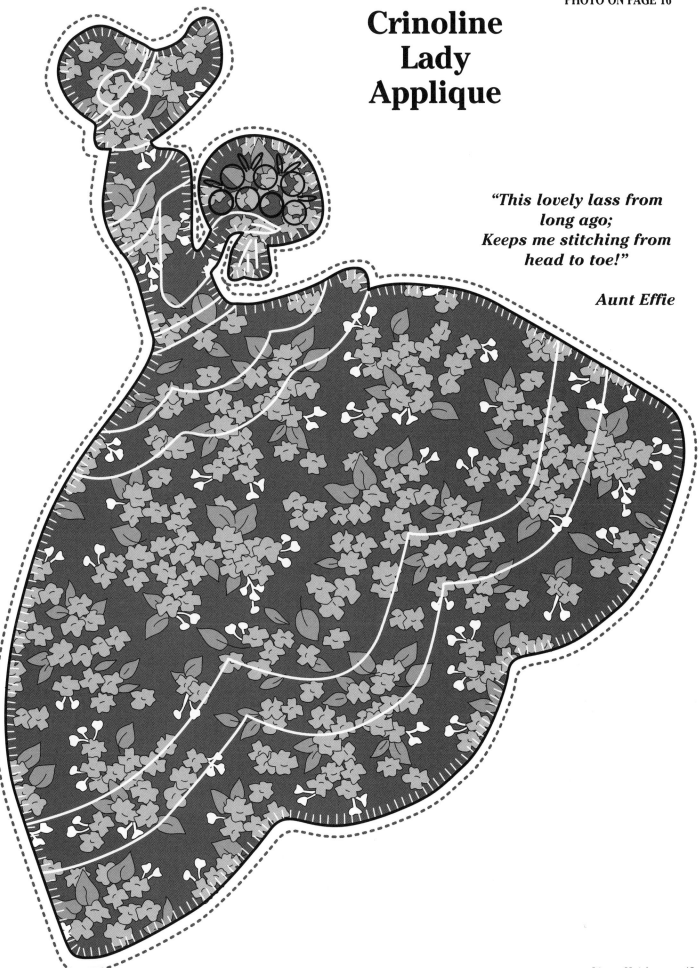

*"This lovely lass from long ago;
Keeps me stitching from head to toe!"*

Aunt Effie

Refer to the instructions on page 35 to tint areas of the design.

God Bless
Our Home

PHOTO ON PAGES 10-11

Flower Bouquet

Refer to the instructions on page 35 to tint areas of the design.

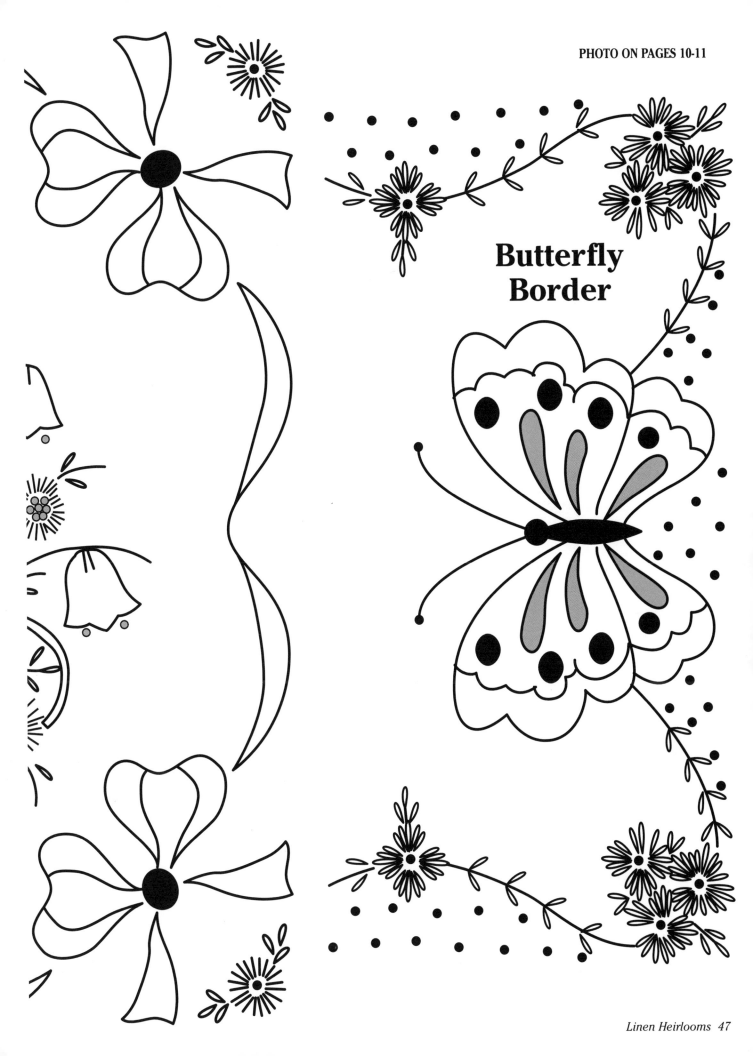

Butterfly Border

Donkey and Flower Cart

Refer to the instructions on page 35 to tint areas of the design.

Stitch Sampler
Flower Bouquet

"As swift and silvery her needle goes
Threaded with amber, sapphire blue and rose
We see upon the fabric snowy white
Flowers of grace and beauty flowing bright."
Viola Perry Wanger
Home Arts, 1936

"No home is complete without a sampler."
Ann Orr Design ad
Modern Priscilla February, 1927

'Days of the Week' Ladies

"I longed to write a noted book, But what I did - was learn to cook. For life with simple tasks is filled."

WASH ON-MONDAY

"And I have done not what I willed Yet when I see boys' hungry eyes, I'm glad I made good apple pies!"

Woman's World, 1928

IRON ON-TUESDAY

SEW
ON-WEDNESDAY

'Days of the Week'
Ladies

"And I have done not what I willed
Yet when I see boys' hungry eyes,
I'm glad I made good apple pies!"

Woman's World, 1928

VISIT
ON-THURSDAY

CLEAN
ON-FRIDAY

BAKE
ON-SATURDAY

*"I wish I were a
Sunbonnet Baby,
With nothing else to do,
But just to live
in Storyland,
And play a whole book
through!"*

CHURCH
ON-SUNDAY

Monday • Tuesday

Wednesday • Thursday

Friday • Saturday

Sunday

'Days of the Week' Best Friends

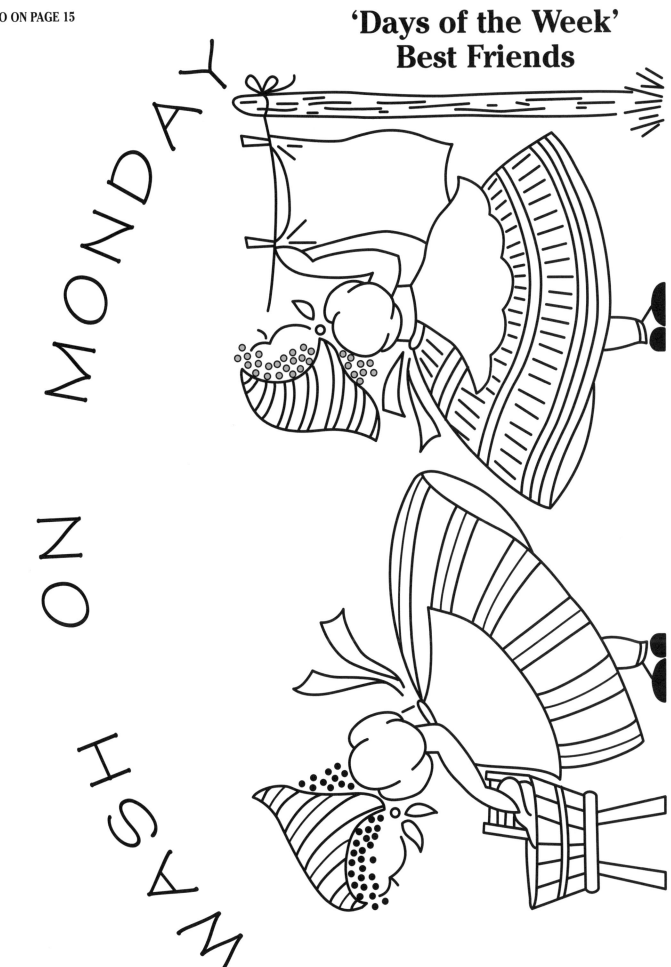

WASH ON MONDAY

'Days of the Week'
Best Friends

IRON ON TUESDAY

MEND ON WEDNESDAY

MARKET ON THURSDAY

'Days of the Week'
Best Friends

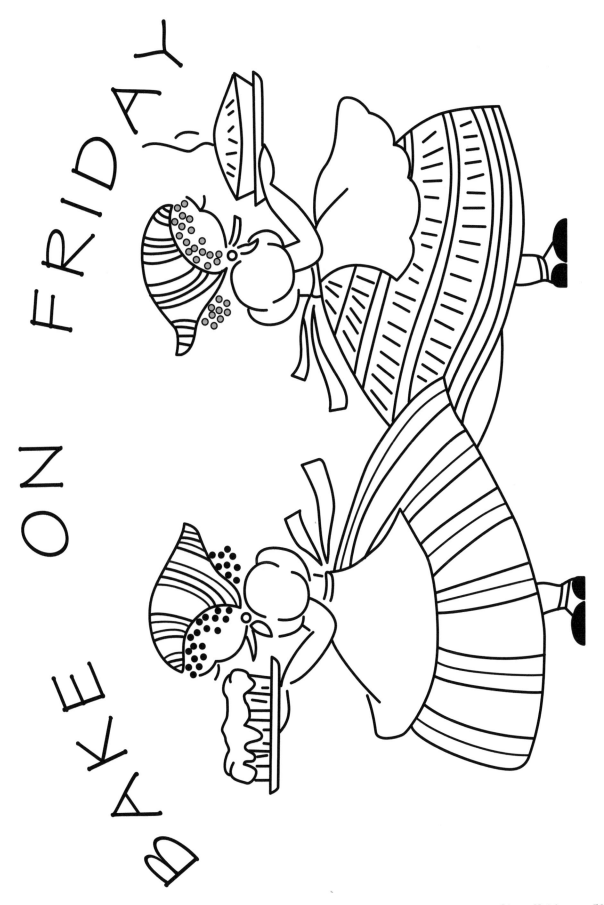

FRIDAY

BAKE ON

CLEAN ON SATURDAY

'Days of the Week' Best Friends

CHURCH ON SUNDAY

'Happy Days' Kitten

PHOTOS ON PAGE 15

'Days of the Week' Kittens

*"It takes
no more time to
embroider these
playful pussies
onto your
kitchen towels
than it does
to read
a light book -
and the pleasure
is every bit
as complete!"*

Book of Needle Arts
circa 1947

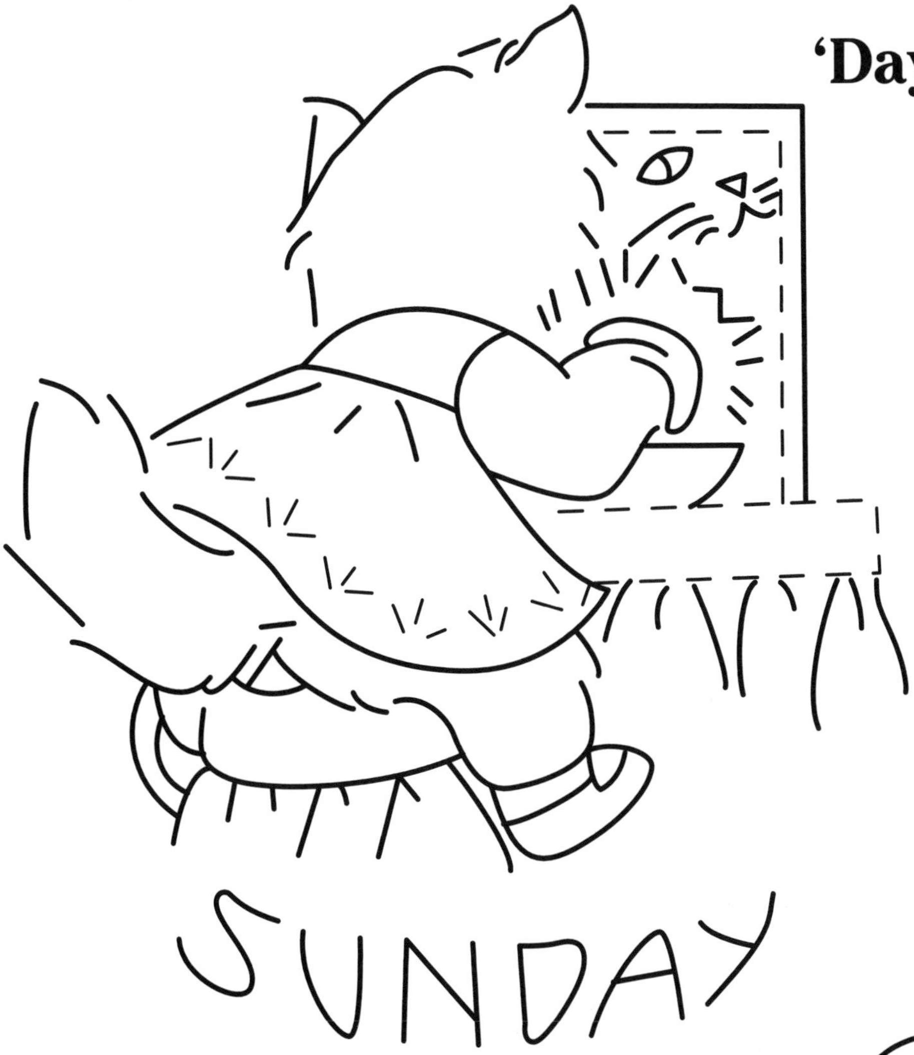
SUNDAY

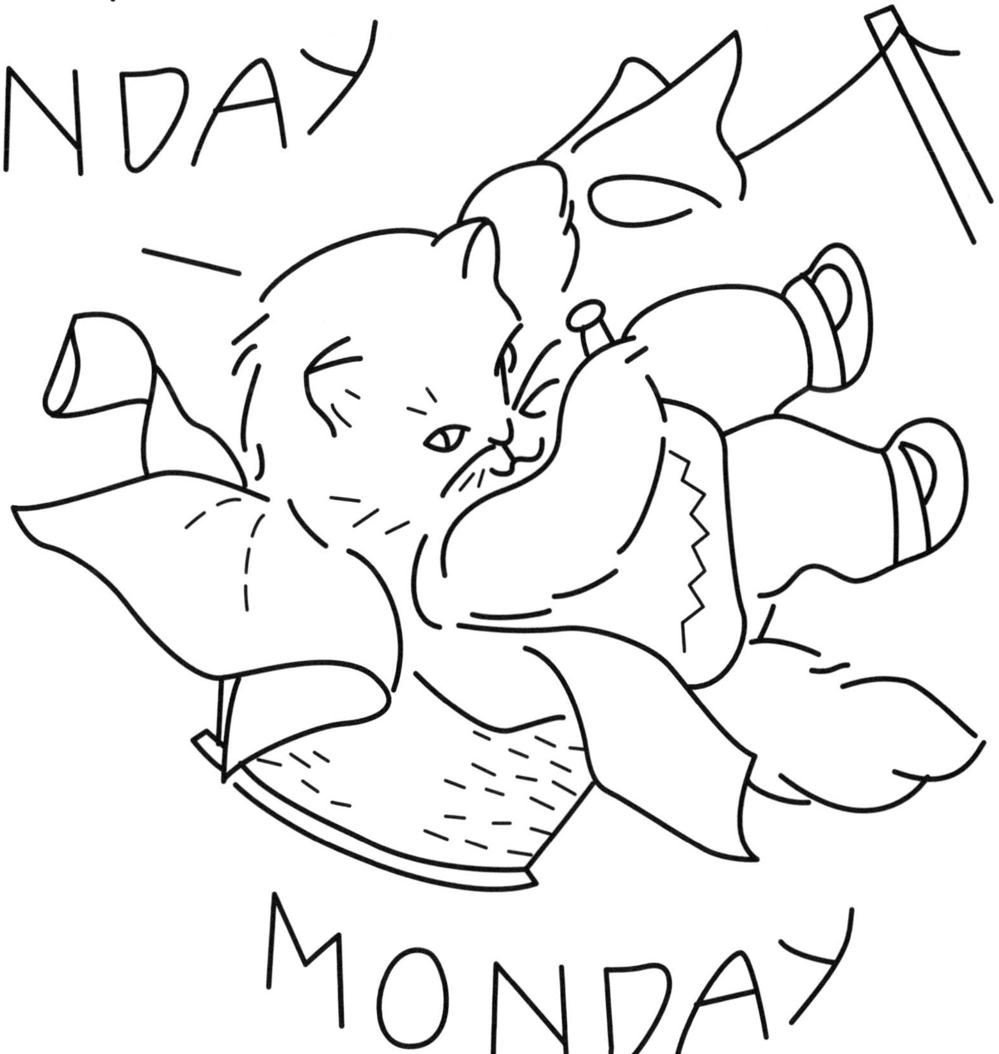
MONDAY

TUESDAY

*"And soon
through the pages,
I dream what
I shall make,
And when they
all are finished,
I from my
daydreams wake..."*

Hazel B. Clarke

WEDNESDAY

'Days of the Week' Kittens

THURSDAY

FRIDAY

'Days of the Week' Kittens

SATURDAY

Home is where your ❤ is.

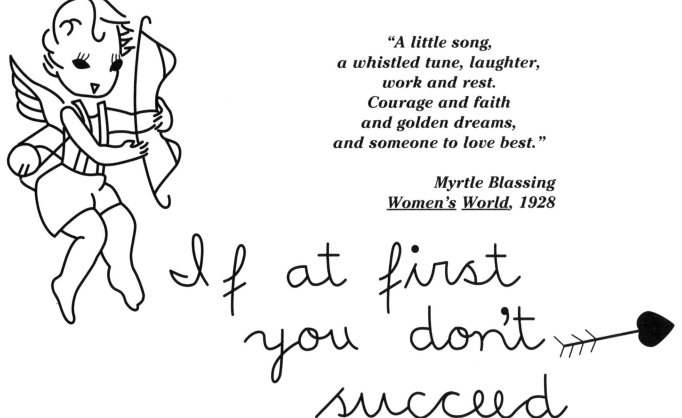

"A little song,
a whistled tune, laughter,
work and rest.
Courage and faith
and golden dreams,
and someone to love best."

Myrtle Blassing
Women's World, 1928

'Love' Borders

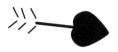

*"And when holes show
in these stockings,
either in the heel or toe,
I must learn
to neatly darn them,
over, under,
to and fro."*

Aunt Effie

MONDAY AH IS HAPPY

Monday's child is fair of face

TUESDAY AH DIS CRY

WEDNESDAY AH IS LAZY

THURSDAY AH IS SHY

Tuesday's child is full of grace

Wednesday's child is full of woe

**'Days of
the Week'
Children**

FRIDAY AH IS SASSY

Thursday's child has far to go

Friday's child is loving & giving

SATURDAY AH IS WISE

Saturday's child works for a living

A child born on the Sabbath Day

'Days of the Week' Children

BUT MAMMY ON A SUNDAY
AH'S AN ANGEL IN DISGUISE

Is fair and wise, good and gay.

**Rooster
and
Hen**

*I rule
the
Roost*

*I rule
the
Rooster*

I rule the Roost

PHOTO ON PAGE 14

I rule the Rooster

Which came first...
the 🐤 or the 🥚?

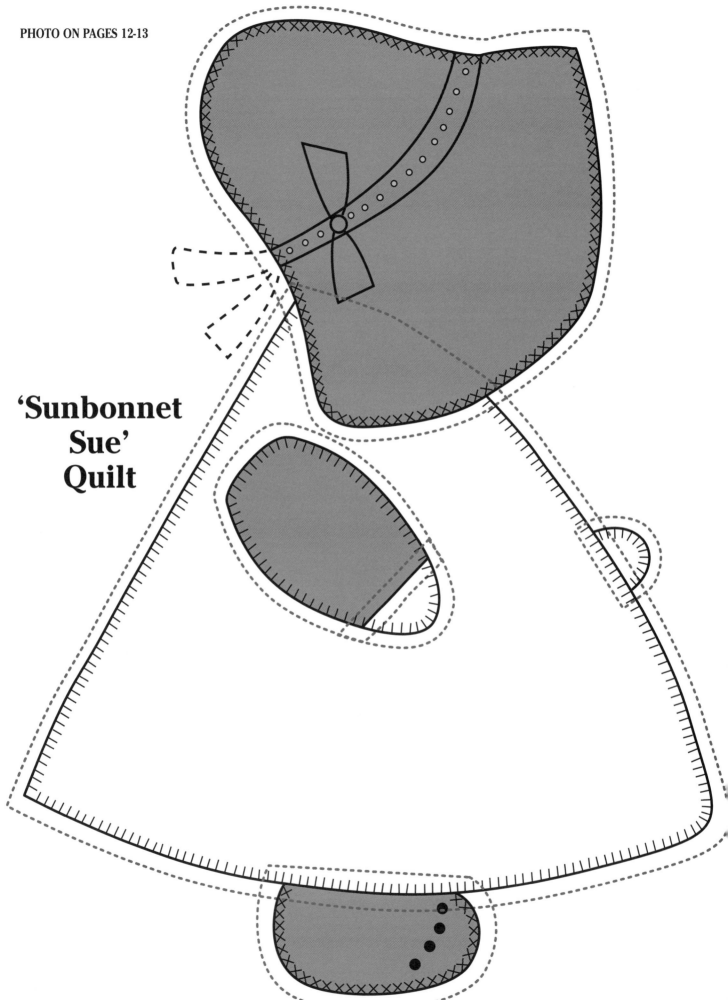

'Sunbonnet Sue' Quilt

Assembly:

1. Fold the plain back circle of the hotpad in half to locate the bottom center. Mark 1" away on either side of the center mark along the seam line on the right side of the circle.

2. For each ruffle, cut a $3^1/2$" x 24" piece of Red fabric. Fold the strip in half along the length, right sides facing. Round off both ends of the strip. Using $1/4$" seam allowance, sew along the rounded ends to close them. Turn the strip to the right side.

3. Make Running stitches through both layers of the strip along the raw edges. Pin one end at one of the marks on the back circle of the hotpad, aligning raw edges of both pieces. Pull the stitches to gather the ruffle evenly around the outer edges of the circle to end at the mark on the other side of center. Pin or baste the ruffle in position. Layer the hotpad front on top of the back/ruffle pieces. Make certain that the bottom of the embroidered design is at the bottom. Sew front to back, leaving a $1^1/2$" opening at the bottom. Turn pieces to the right side. Sew the opening closed.

4. For the bow, cut a $1^1/4$" x 14" strip of Red fabric. Fold the strip in half along the length, right sides facing.Using $1/4$" seam allowance, sew along one end and down the straight edge. Leave the other end open. Turn the strip to the right side. Fold back seam allowances and sew the other end closed. Tie the strip into a bow and sew it at the bottom center of the hotpad.

Potholders

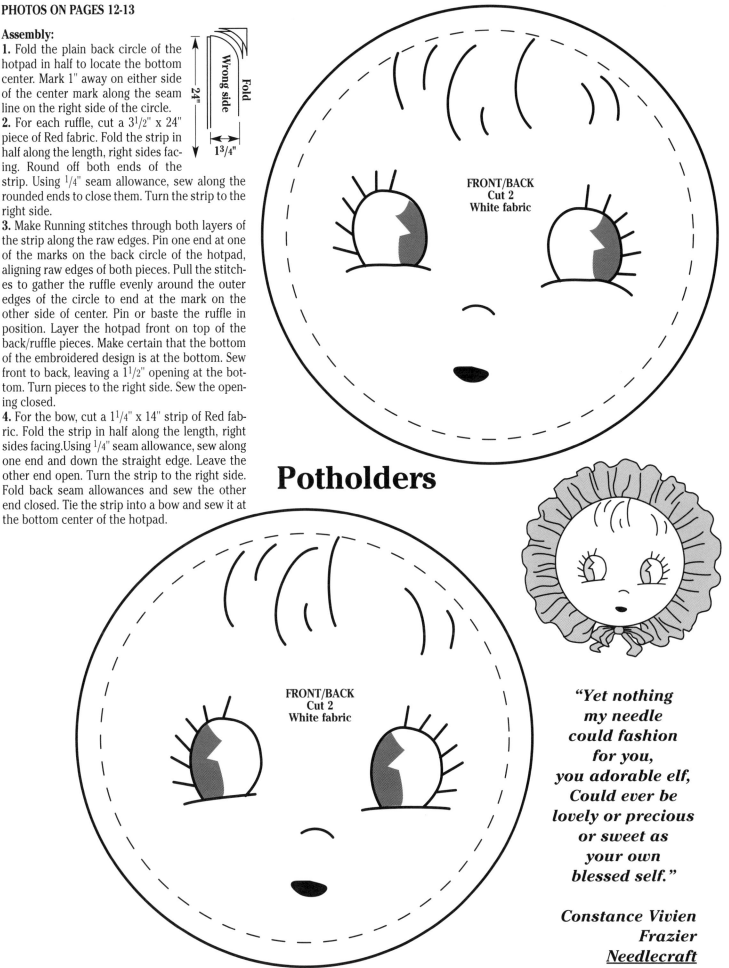

FRONT/BACK
Cut 2
White fabric

FRONT/BACK
Cut 2
White fabric

"Yet nothing my needle could fashion for you, you adorable elf, Could ever be lovely or precious or sweet as your own blessed self."

Constance Vivien Frazier Needlecraft

Sunbonnet Girl

What linen collection would be complete
without a sunbonnet quilt?
The timeless attraction of these little girls
is not hard to understand.
Maybe that bit of shyness is what touches our hearts.
Whatever the allure, the sunbonnet has been
a standard theme in needlework
since 1900.

Silverware Girl

Girl in Pantaloons

"Here's to fun and frolic in the kitchen!"

Pattern envelope circa 1947

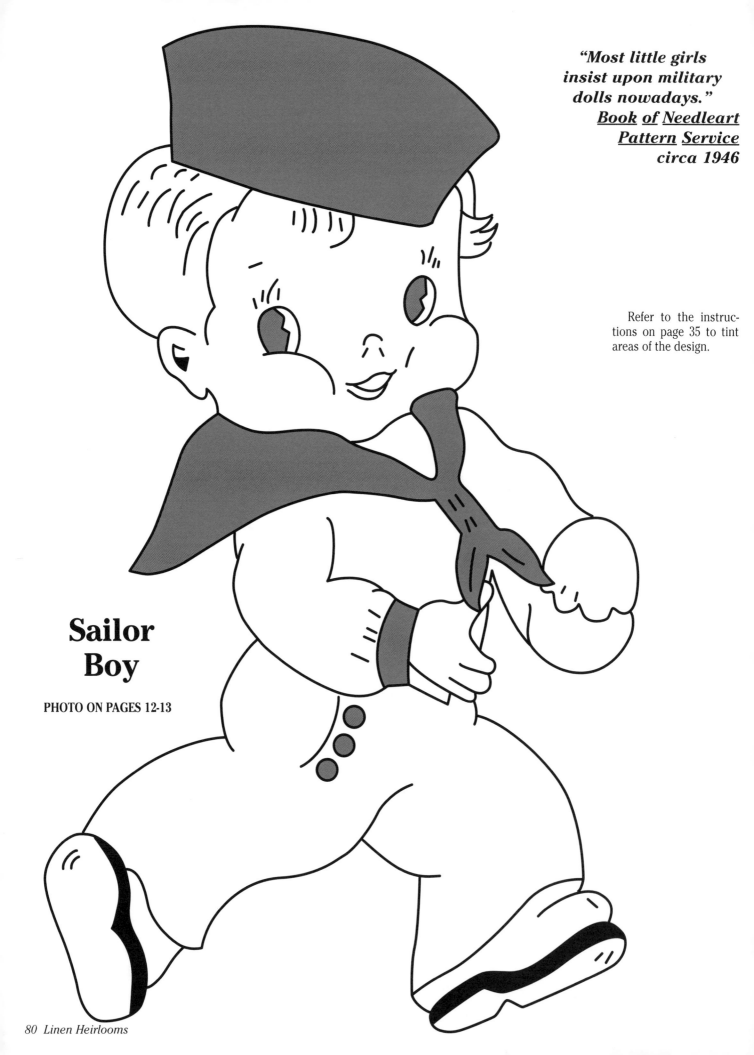

"Most little girls insist upon military dolls nowadays."
__Book__ __of__ __Needleart__
__Pattern__ __Service__
circa 1946

Refer to the instructions on page 35 to tint areas of the design.

Sailor Boy

PHOTO ON PAGES 12-13

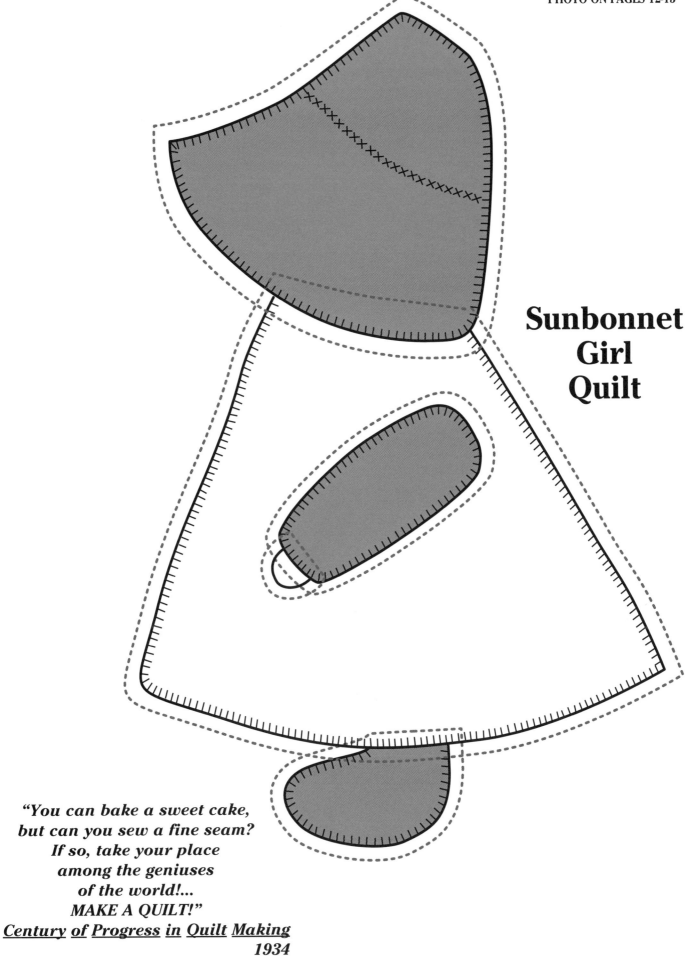

Sunbonnet Girl Quilt

"You can bake a sweet cake, but can you sew a fine seam? If so, take your place among the geniuses of the world!... MAKE A QUILT!"
<u>Century</u> <u>of</u> <u>Progress</u> <u>in</u> <u>Quilt</u> <u>Making</u>
1934

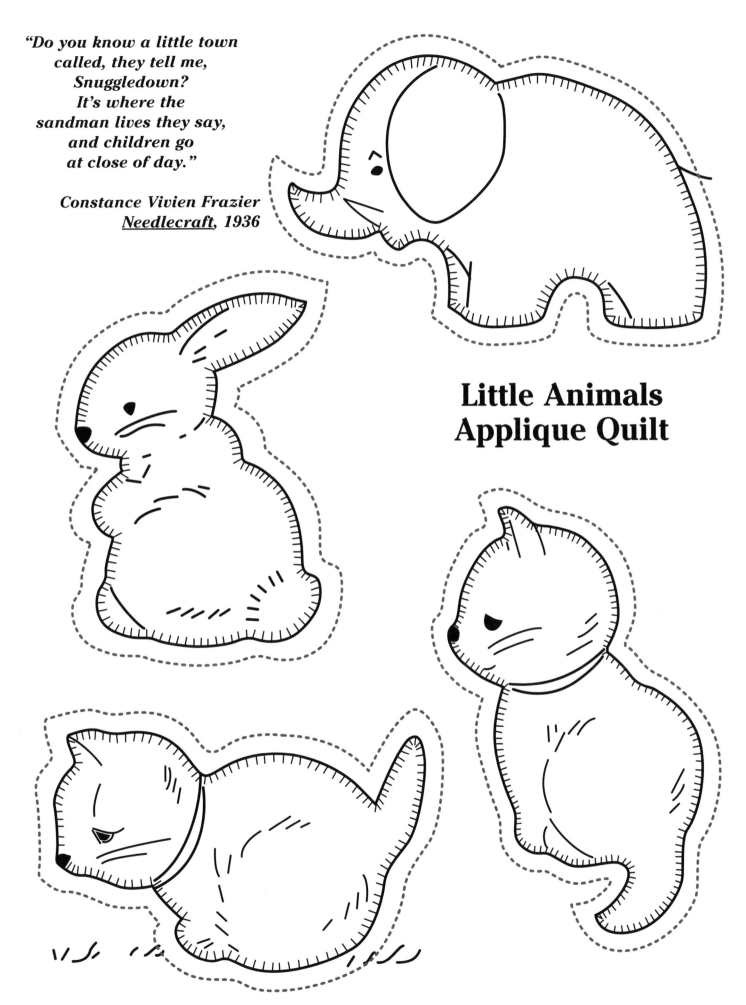

"Do you know a little town called, they tell me, Snuggledown? It's where the sandman lives they say, and children go at close of day."

Constance Vivien Frazier
<u>Needlecraft</u>, 1936

Little Animals Applique Quilt

Clown Puppy
Quilt

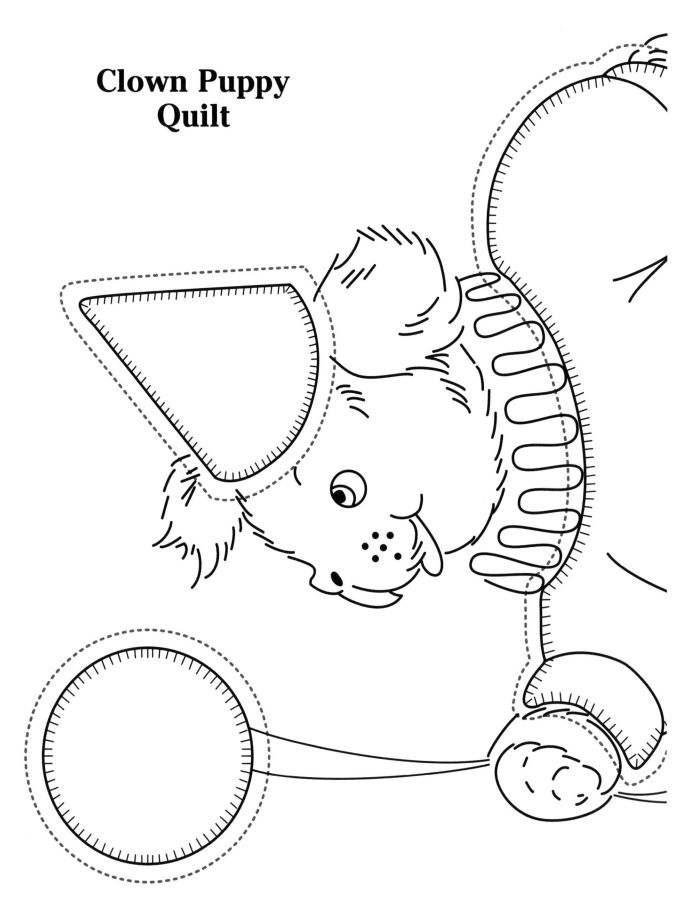

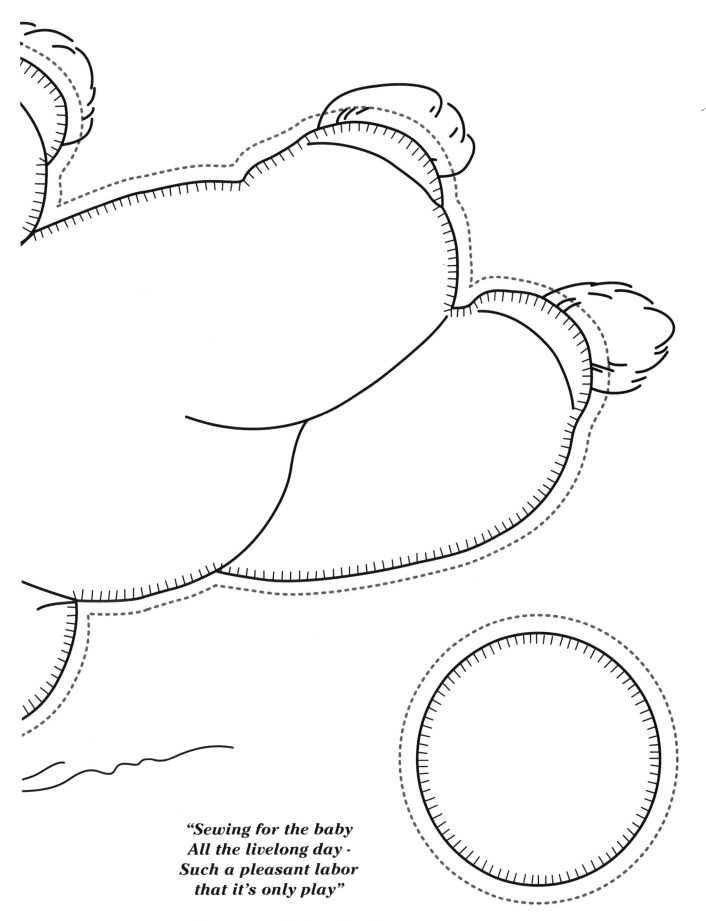

"Sewing for the baby
All the livelong day -
Such a pleasant labor
that it's only play"

Constance Vivien Frazier

Puppy
and Kitten

PHOTO ON PAGES 8-9

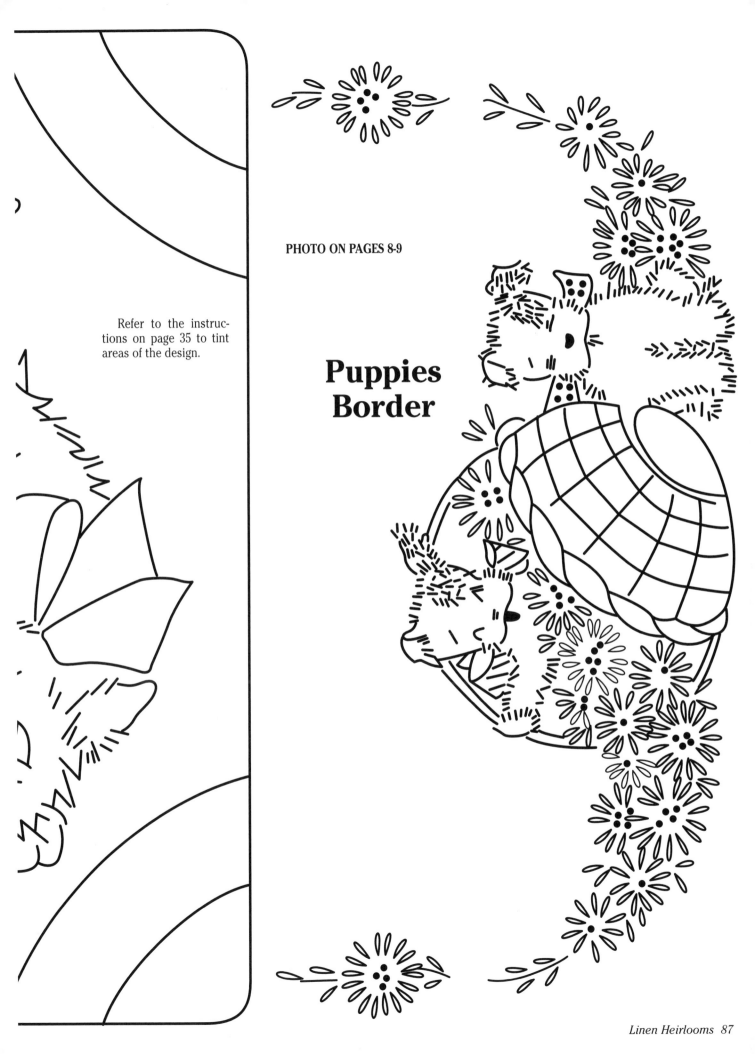

PHOTO ON PAGES 8-9

Refer to the instruc-
tions on page 35 to tint
areas of the design.

Puppies
Border

*"A scotty dog
stopped at home
With open door,
no more he'll roam;
He's made his bed
beside my chair
And through the years,
he'll slumber there."*

Aunt Effie

Scotty Dog and Kitten

Puppy in a Car

Refer to the instructions on page 35 to tint areas of the design.

A

B

PHOTO ON PAGES 8-9

Puppy Applique Potholder

*"A scottish pup I'll stitch for you,
a little guardian brave and true."*

Aunt Effie

'Topsy Turvy' Spotted Puppies in Cups

Refer to the instructions on page 35 to tint areas of the design.

PHOTOS ON PAGES 8-9

*"What is worse
than naughty pups
spilling cream
and breaking cups"*

Aunt Effie

Gingham Cat

"The gingham dog and the calico cat
side by side on the table sat...
The dog went 'bow-wow-wow,'
and the cat replied 'meow.'"

Playful Kitten

Refer to the instructions on page 35 to tint areas of the design.

PHOTO ON PAGE 99

*"Pretty things for baby,
For carriage, crib and chair -
Dainty things to cover him,
Pretty things to wear."*

Constance Vivien Frazier

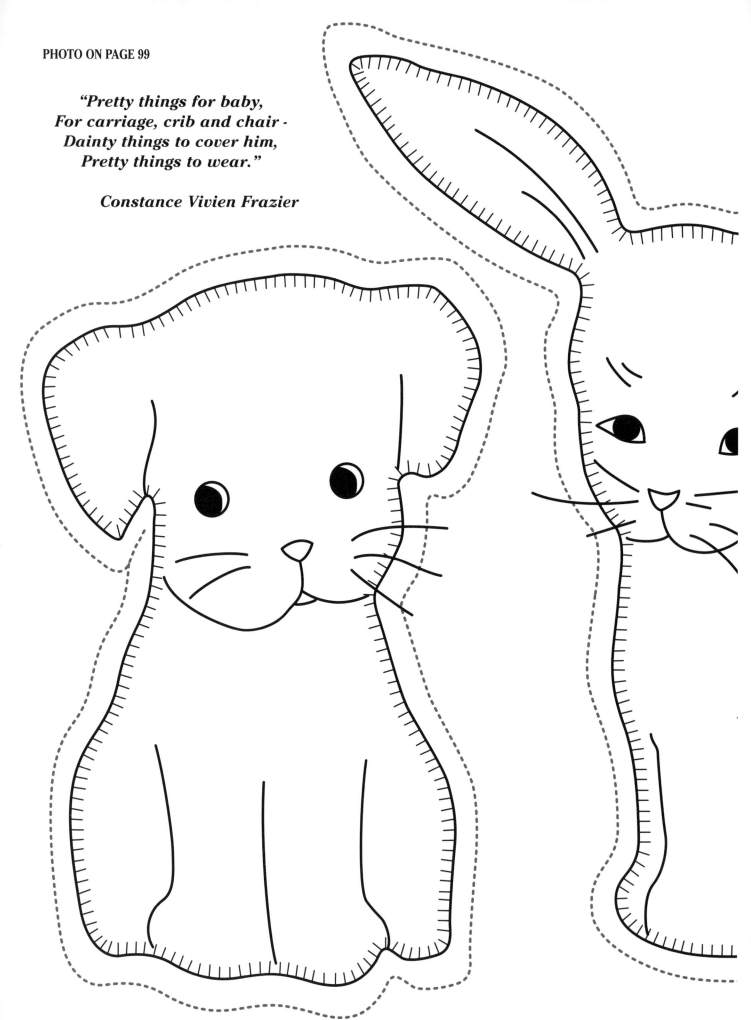

Playful Animals
Applique Quilt

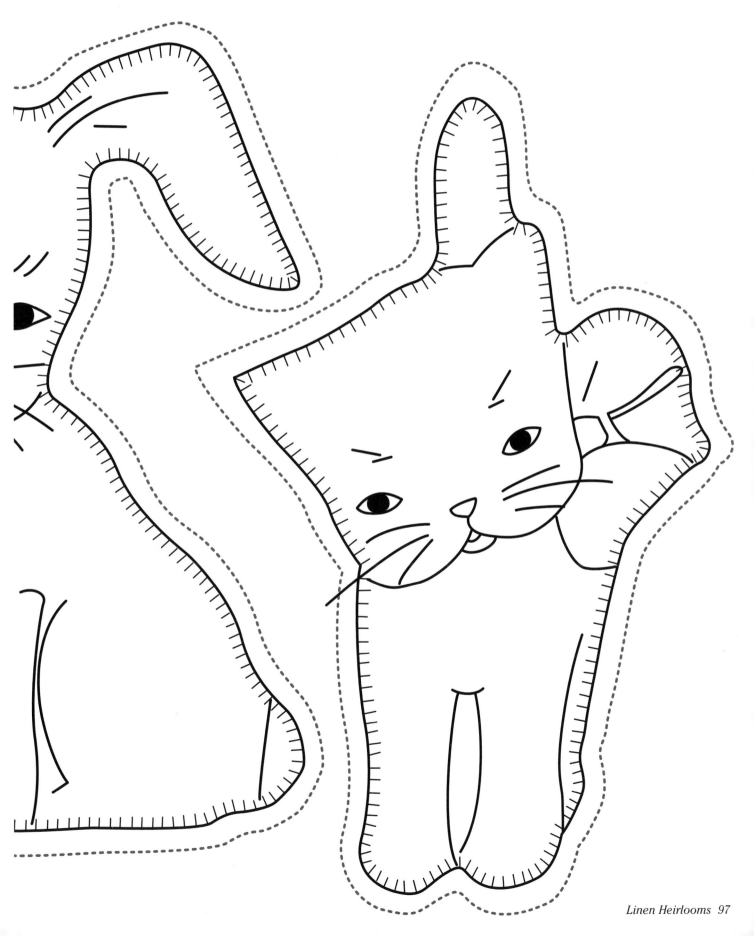

Estimating Pattern Age

Without a dated envelope or other dated source illustrating a pattern, there is no fool-proof way to tell a pattern's age. Pattern companies tended to sell popular patterns for as long as they could. One large pattern manufacturer admitted they were still selling (in 1993) a design originally published in the 1920s!

It isn't uncommon to observe the same pattern for sale, from catalog to catalog or magazine to magazine, over the course of 10, 20 or even 40 years. Keeping this in mind, it is certainly possible to estimate the general age of a pattern by observing a few simple elements.

Is it a perforated pattern?

You have a real treasure. Perforated patterns for embroidery were most popular before the turn of the century, and a little after. (Some companies continued to make them into the 'teens, but transfers were by far the most popular by that time. Decide what time period the designs seem closest to by looking at the previous charts for helpful style information.

Is the pattern printed on tissue or paper?

Only a few pattern companies used paper for transfer patterns before WWII; most preferred tissue. Some companies continued to print on tissue after the war, however. Often, this post-war tissue is more brittle than tissue from the 1920s or earlier. By the 1950s, the majority of patterns were on paper.

What color is the ink?

Early transfer patterns were generally printed in blue or blue grey; they also came in yellow. Around WWII and just afterwards, some companies switched from blue to a green ink which has a pronounced, raised appearance. Other companies (Monarch especially) used a silver ink; red was used by several of the largest companies. Blue remained popular.

Are the lines dotted, continuous or flaking?

Dotted patterns indicate that your pattern is from before 1930; most likely it is from before 1925. These dots are a wax transfer which melted into a continuous line when heat was applied. A continuous Blue line which shows a lot of flaking is another strong sign of age, probably before 1930. Continuous lines without substantial flaking are likely from after 1930, although you may just be lucky in finding a much older pattern in remarkably good shape!

Is there a name on the pattern?

Names like Standard, Designer, Royal Society and Kaumgraph (the original McCall's name) all indicate a pattern from before 1925. Walter's may be anywhere from the turn of the century to the late 1940s. There were at least a dozen notable pattern companies before WWII. Not many survived past the 1950s. Names like Laura Wheeler, Alice Brooks and Old Chelsea Station were subscription pattern services popular from the late 1940s until the early 1960s. American Thread and Vogart distributed patterns from the late 1940s until the '60s and '70s, respectively.

Is the style of the design consistent with the age the other elements suggest?

Generally speaking, the more polished looking the artwork on a pattern, the more recent it is. Patterns from the late 1930s onwards have a distinctly professional look, almost reminiscent of a wonderful cartoon. Look out, though! A few companies - Joseph Walker in particular - specialized in beautifully drawn patterns, full of tiny details and superb rendering. Often it is the details in these patterns which give away their age. Remember, though, your pattern may have been drawn 10 years before the copy you hold in your hand was purchased by its original owner!

Baby Animal Baby Coverlet

FINISHED SIZE: 35½" x 46"

MATERIALS:
- 44" wide, 100% cotton fabrics:
  2 yards White fabric for blocks and backing
  1¼ yards Pink fabric for the kitten appliques, blocks and borders
  2 Blue 9" squares for the dog appliques
  2 Light Yellow 9" squares for the bunny appliques
- 3 skeins of Dark Gray embroidery floss
- White sewing thread

CUTTING:
- Cut 6 White 11" squares.
- Cut 6 Pink 11" squares.
- Cut 2 Pink 9" squares for the kitten appliques.
- Cut 2 Pink 2¼" x 42½" strips for the side borders.
- Cut 2 Pink 2¼" x 36" strips for the top and bottom borders.
- Cut 1 White 36" x 47" piece for the backing.

DESIGN BLOCKS:

Transfer one of each of the designs on pages 96 and 97 to the appropriate 9" squares. Reverse the designs and transfer one of each of the designs to the appropriate color square. Cut along the dotted line. Turn back the seam allowance and trim curves as necessary. Pin or baste the shapes onto the center of a White square. Use 2 strands of floss to blanket stitch the edges in place. Remove the basting stitches or pins. Add stitching details. Press each square.

MANY THANKS to my friends for their cheerful help and wonderful ideas!
Production Director - Kathy McMillan
Art Director - Jen Tennyson
Assistant Art Director - Marti Wyble
Graphic Artist - Charlie Davis/Young
Photography - David & Donna Thomason